Managing So*twa*

Managing Software Engineering

CASE studies and solutions

Alan C. Gillies

and

Peter Smith

CHAPMAN & HALL

London · Glasgow · Weinheim · New York · Tokyo · Melbourne · Madras

Published by Chapman & Hall, 2-6 Boundary Row, London SE1 8HN, UK

Chapman & Hall, 2-6 Boundary Row, London SE1 8HN, UK

Blackie Academic & Professional, Wester Cleddens Road, Bishopbriggs, Glasgow G64 2NZ, UK

Chapman & Hall GmbH, Pappelallee 3, 69469 Weinheim, Germany

Chapman & Hall USA, One Penn Plaza, 41st Floor, New York, NY10119, USA

Chapman & Hall Japan, ITP-Japan, Kyowa Building, 3F, 2-2-1 Hirakawacho, Chiyoda-ku, Tokyo 102, Japan

Chapman & Hall Australia, Thomas Nelson Australia, 102 Dodds Street, South Melbourne, Victoria 3205, Australia

Chapman & Hall India, R. Seshadri, 32 Second Main Road, CIT East, Madras 600 035, India

First edition 1994

© 1994 Alan C. Gillies and Peter Smith

Printed in Great Britain by St Edmundsbury Press, Bury St Edmunds, Suffolk

ISBN   0 412   56550 1

A catalogue record for this book is available from the British Library

∞ Printed on permanent acid-free text paper, manufactured in accordance with ANSI/NISO Z39.48-1992 and ANSI/NISO Z39.48-1984 (Permanence of Paper).

Contents

1

Introduction

1.1 WHAT THE BOOK IS ABOUT

This book is about building computer software. The aim of the book is to highlight the lessons from previous experience. Thus, you will not find detailed descriptions of specific methods and tools such as SSADM or Excelerator here. Instead, the book will describe other people's experiences in software development and try to distil some of the knowledge that they have gained.

The main hypothesis underpinning the text is that although software development methods and supporting tools have become more technically sophisticated, the management knowledge required has failed to keep pace. Further, technically sophisticated tools and proprietary 'methodologies' have been presented by suppliers as substitutes for sound project management practice.

Thus, the book will emphasize the importance of managing the software development process and suggest that modern methods and tools place a greater emphasis upon sound management practice rather than less.

1.2 WHAT'S IN THE BOOK

The book is arranged as a chronological tale from the origins of software engineering up to the present and looking to the future. However, the book is divided in three sections to assist the reader in finding the material that they require:

- Part One deals with the historical development of software engineering. It describes the development of the principal ideas in software engineering and outlines how we have arrived at the current situation.

- Part Two describes the state of Computer Aided Software Engineering (CASE) in the UK up to 1991, based upon two major studies. The first is the DTI Solutions programme organized by Salford University Business Services Limited. The aim of this programme was to raise the awareness of CASE methods and tools amongst small and medium sized companies. In the process, the SOLUTIONS team collected a valuable collection of experiences from companies who have implemented software methods and tools. Many of these are presented in this text as case studies illustrating the later chapters of the book. The report on this study has been kindly contributed by John Kirkham of the IT Institute, Salford, who was director of the Solutions programme. The second study was a survey of the uptake of CASE in the UK carried out by the University of Sunderland. The survey highlighted that many companies had experienced problems in making practical use of the methods and tools.

- Part Three draws upon the findings of the two studies. It attempts to draw out the lessons to be learnt from the experiences of the companies contacted by the two studies. Each chapter focuses upon a specific aspect of developing software and is based upon a central principle.

The book is intended for a broad audience since the authors believe that both technical and management personnel must recognize the need for managing the software process. However, the organization into distinct parts is intended to cater for different readers' needs.

For the student, at undergraduate or postgraduate level, it is suggested that they will benefit from reading the whole text, since Part One provides a foundation for Part Two, and Part Three is based upon the findings of the studies in Part Two.

However, technical people already familiar with the history of software development may wish to start reading at Part Two. Those wishing to find out more about managing the software process or whether other people have experienced the same problem that they face may confine their attentions to Part Three.

PART ONE

THE STORY SO FAR

2

A brief history of software

2.1 THE DARK AGES

In the early days of computers, programming was considered to be something of a black art, performed by mad scientists who were clever enough (and probably mad enough) to program these strange beasts of technology known as computers. These scientists sat for endless hours ploughing through strange computer codes known as programs which were, undoubtedly, incomprehensible to anyone but themselves. These early programmers did not follow any methods or rules when constructing their programs; rather they applied their high intellects to the problem in a way that lesser mortals could not be expected to achieve.

The truth of the matter was that programming was difficult in those times, not least because of the fact that, in the very early days, no real programming languages existed. However, languages such as FORTRAN and COBOL soon did emerge, but they were not accompanied by any disciplined or formalized approaches to software development. In addition, there were no effective tools available to help the programmer in his/her task.

Thus programs tended to be thrown together in a haphazard manner, with no real attention being paid to trying to structure them. The prime objective in those days was to produce a program that was efficient and could be squeezed into as small an amount of computer storage as possible, as at that time the cost of computer power was quite prohibitive.

This sort of approach seemed to work quite well, without causing too many disasters for a number of years. As long as the mad scientists got the right results (or rather, a set of results that appeared to be right) they remained happy, and convinced that their program was correct. These happy days were not, however, to last for long.

Soon managers, computer users and all sorts of people were demanding, and indeed expecting, a lot more from the computer. They had had a taste of what the computer could do for them and wanted more. At the same time, the programmers and their bosses were becoming more imaginative and adventurous. Thus much more complex and large pieces of software were being developed. Large operating systems for the new generations of computers were being developed. However, no-one really understood the best way to approach the development of such complex software products. Nor did they have any tools that could help them put together these pieces of software. As program size grew, so complexity increased and the need to manage that complexity increased. In the absence of appropriate tools and methods to manage complexity, the number of errors began to accelerate and the cost of fixing those errors, euphemistically referred to as 'maintenance', increased out of control.

This was the point at which real problems began to arise.

- Software projects were taking a lot longer to finish than originally envisaged.

- Software was costing a lot more to develop than initially imagined.

- Software was being delivered to the customer only to fail (i.e. produce incorrect results).

- Software projects were being abandoned because of disastrous failures.

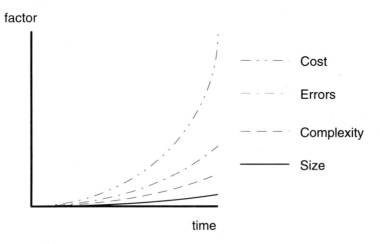

Fig. 2.1 The software crisis.

In summary, software failures were costing an unacceptable amount of money, and it was this that forced the software development community to rethink their working practices. This became known as the 'software crisis'. The proposed solution was to borrow ideas about systematic development from another discipline, that of engineering.

2.2 THE ENGINEERING APPROACH

The term 'software engineering' was first coined in the late 1960s for the application of ideas on systematic development from engineering disciplines. Let us consider first a problem from civil engineering.

Consider a gang of labourers who have had no training in bricklaying, plumbing, electrical work, or any of the activities needed to build a house. This gang of labourers have, however, managed to fumble their way through building a few small houses. The houses don't look great and may not be very comfortable: but at least they don't fall down and you can live in them. The leader of the gang is confident that they can build houses and feels that the time is right to attempt a more ambitious project.

On Monday morning, without any warning, the leader informs the gang that they are going to build a skyscraper. The gang start piling bricks on top of each other, without any real thought about what they are doing. Soon they are running into real difficulties, as the skyscraper begins to wobble about, and ultimately it crashes to the ground!

This is, of course, an example of how not to go about constructing a building (or indeed anything else). A true engineer (because it is engineering that we are discussing) would surely approach the problem in a much more systematic and professional manner. They would use methods, techniques, standards and tools to aid in the production process.

The type of disaster described above is, however, the very situation which had arisen in the software industry. A number of largely untrained (or, at the best, self-trained) programmers would attempt to throw together a very large and complex piece of software without following any rules or guidelines, or attempting to apply any real methods. They would not plan out their work to any great extent, nor would they make any real estimate of the consequences of their actions. What is being described is, of course, a recipe for disaster – and that is exactly what happened in a large number of instances. It is this scenario that leads us to the emergence of the concept of software engineering.

2.3   THE ADVENT OF SOFTWARE ENGINEERING

The purpose of software engineering is clear. It may be defined as:

'The application of traditional engineering approaches to the development of software'.

In practice, the engineering approach is characterized principally by the application of a systematic method to the problem in hand. A general engineering method which all engineers might recognize would include:

- establishment of clear goals;

- a clear plan, breaking down the overall problem into a set of simpler tasks;

- use of a systematic method to control and manage the project;

- use of suitable tools to support the process;

- evaluation and monitoring of the process;

- testing of the materials used and the product.

Within the overall sphere of engineering there are many distinct disciplines, such as civil, mechanical, electrical and chemical. What they share is an overall systematic approach to problems in the same way that a chemist, biologist or physicist would recognize that they have scientific method in common.

However, the difference between most engineering disciplines is small when compared to the differences between physical engineering disciplines and software engineering.

The crucial characteristic of software is its intangibility. You cannot hit software with a hammer. More importantly, perhaps, you cannot measure it with a ruler or micrometer or adjust it with a screwdriver. Much of engineering theory and practice depends upon measurement. Software measures are at best very crude and much less objective than their counterparts in other engineering disciplines:

Fig. 2.2 Software cannot easily be measured.

Nevertheless, it is still a product; an item which humans make. The idea behind software engineering is, then, that software should be engineered, in as professional a manner as a civil engineer might construct a bridge or an automotive engineer might construct a car.

In particular, software engineering implies the use of tools, techniques and methods for the production of quality software. That is, the software engineer must approach the construction of their product, software, in a professional manner. Their work should, therefore, involve adherence to standards, quality control procedures and professional practices. Software production should be carefully managed from the highest level with each software engineer clear of their own responsibilities and taking a pride in their work.

All of this is, of course, a very fine ideal. When these ideas were proposed they certainly seemed a long way from reality. Everyone agreed that it would be wonderful if software engineers could adhere to such practices; few people had the vision to imagine how this might be achieved.

It was difficult (and still is) to imagine or predict the answers to the following questions:

• How do you measure the quality of software?

• How can you provide tools to aid in software construction?

• How can you plan complex software projects?

• How can you devise methods to aid in software design?

The past two decades have seen much research effort (and money) go into answering the above, and other, important questions in the field of software engineering. We have undoubtedly come a long way in that period and many methods, tools and techniques have arisen. CASE tools are one very important part of this scenario.

Some of these methods and tools are now in wide usage in business and commerce; others are still very much at the research stage. One thing is, however, without question – software development has been raised from what was a somewhat haphazard cottage industry into a professional discipline. Whether it is worthy of the title 'Software Engineering' is still a matter for some debate; but the term is now in common usage.

The concept of professionalism is at the very heart of software engineering, and CASE tools must, if they do anything useful at all, raise the level of professionalism in the software development community. In the UK, members of computing's professional body can now apply for chartered status, which signifies their recognition as a professional engineer. Some people, including traditional engineers in other disciplines, would, however, argue that computing is still too immature a discipline to warrant being termed 'engineering' and that there are still too few methods, tools, techniques and quality assurance procedures being applied in industry and commerce.

The process of software engineering is dealt with comprehensively in a text by Sommerville (1989).

2.4   THE SOFTWARE LIFE CYCLE

At the heart of any engineering process is a systematic procedure consisting of a number of stages from initial conception through to the final finished article. These stages are commonly termed the software life cycle. The primary role of CASE tools is to support and automate all or part of the life cycle. The stages in the software life cycle are:

- Analysis

- Design

- Implementation (Coding)

- Testing

- Installation

- Maintenance.

Each of these stages must be managed, documented and validated.

Each stage of the software life cycle will be considered in more detail below.

2.4.1 Analysis

This stage consists of analysing the user's problems, and is one of the most difficult, creative and intuitive stages in the software development process. It is also one of the most difficult areas to automate and, hence, is less well supported by current tools than later stages of the life cycle.

The questions to be answered at this stage may include:

- What is the real problem to be solved?

- What do the potential users of the software need?

- What computer and programs are needed?

- What data is to be used?

- What results are to be presented?

• How are they to be presented?

This stage will involve extensive discussions and consultations with the people who are going to use the software in the future. The best which current tools can do is to support certain aspects of this process, by helping the systems analyst to produce diagrammatic models of the systems and to check the consistency of these models as they are successively refined. The output of this stage will be a detailed specification that will describe exactly:

• the inputs and outputs of the system;

• the hardware and software to be used;

• the functions to be performed by the system;

• the form and structure of the user interface (i.e. how the system is to interact with its users).

The ideal tool would be able to generate automatically such system elements. One of the most useful applications of tools in support of the analysis process is through the use of prototyping to allow users to see the implications of their specific requirements.

Methods and tools have been developed by a number of authors to assist in this process, and the reader is referred to Chapters 3 to 6 of Sommerville's (1989) book for further details.

2.4.2 Design

This stage entails the design of the software. Here the software engineers will decide how many programs need to be written and describe their overall structure.

The major concept underpinning methods and tools for design is structuredness. The idea behind structuredness is to break down the overall problem into a set of simpler tasks. In so doing the process imposes organization onto the problem.

The inputs to this stage of development are the requirements described in the analysis phase. The purpose of this stage is to formalize the requirements into a design, usually expressed as a hierarchical structure of some form:

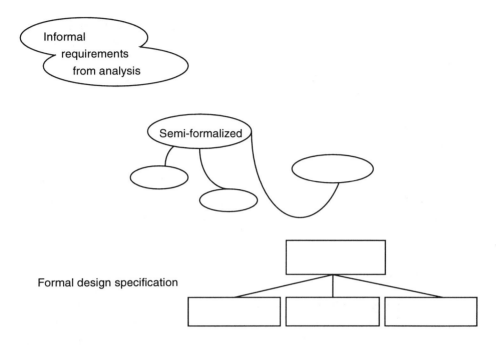

Fig. 2.3 The design process (schematic).

The output from this stage may be expressed in the form of diagrams or text, generally known as a design description language. Increasingly the influence of graphically based tools is switching the emphasis to diagram-based techniques.

The classic methods of structured design were pioneered by authors such as Constantine and Yourdon (1979) and Jackson (1975, 1983).

2.4.3 Implementation

The implementation (or coding) stage involves taking the software design and converting it into the instructions of a programming language, typically in the past this would have been COBOL for business applications and FORTRAN for scientific applications.

However, the growth of structured methods has led to the growth of languages which encourage structured programming such as Pascal and more significantly C and ADA.

In business applications, the use of so-called fourth generation languages (4GL) has become increasingly popular, in order to increase productivity and ease interaction with a database system. Some of these are closely linked to tools to support the rest of the development process such as ORACLE's proprietary 4GL and CASE tool.

The future of implementation will depend increasingly upon the automatic generation of code from design specification. Coding is not essentially a creative process and the most important feature is to consistently mirror the design specification. Thus this is a task well suited to automation.

However, the current generation of tools have limitations and many tools offer only partial code generation. Jackson (1983) describes the principles of structured programming. There is little published literature regarding automatic code generation as yet, but this topic is discussed in Part Three.

2.4.4 Testing

Any quality product is only of high quality if it has been subject to rigorous quality assurance procedures. This entails testing the software as rigorously as possible to ensure that it performs according to specification. As well as testing the product at this late stage, checks and reviews should be built into the software life cycle at every stage. CASE tools can help in this process, in that they can check that as the system is being designed the models that are being developed are consistent with previous views of the system and its domain.

Boehm (1981) highlights the rising cost of error detection throughout the software life cycle. This is illustrated in Fig. 2.4.

Thus, testing and validation must be carried out throughout the software life cycle to detect as many errors as possible at an early stage. CASE tools can assist by providing consistency checks at all stages of the life cycle. A classic text on software testing is provided by Myers (1979).

2.4.5 Installation

Once the software has been fully tested it should be installed on the user's computer. This can be a relatively simple process for small pieces of software, but may be much more complicated for larger, more complex systems. It may also involve training the users of the software exactly how to operate it. The software should also be accompanied by manuals to tell the users how to operate it.

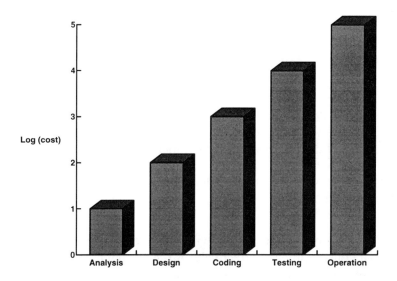

Fig. 2.4 The cost of fixing errors (after Boehm,1981).

In theory, CASE tools can help in the generation of both user and technical documentation. In practice, many tools generate much material relevant to documentation in an unhelpful form.

2.4.6 Maintenance

Now that the software has been installed, it must be maintained. This entails correcting any bugs that the users may subsequently find in the software and ensuring that it continues to work correctly in the future.

This may also involve updating the software to meet new user requirements and changes in the environment in which the software operates. Although CASE cannot help directly in the maintenance process, the use of CASE in software development can help produce more maintainable code.

Since it is alleged that most maintenance arises from badly designed software that does not meet users' requirements effectively, the use of better analysis and design methods and tools should reduce the maintenance required substantially.

This is the reason why CASE methods and tools are presented as a solution to the software crisis. If they cannot do this, then they are being sold to organizations under false pretences.

2.4.7 Continuous activities

Throughout the software life cycle it is necessary to ensure that:

- the software development process is tightly managed and controlled;

- each stage of the process is carefully documented;

- everything produced is validated, including preliminary designs, documents, etc.

The use of a systematic method will help to ensure that these tasks are carried out consistently and effectively. A CASE tool can help to increase productivity by assisting in the production of documentation and diagrams.

However, one of the greatest potential benefits arises from the sharing of data between the different phases of development. A CASE tool uses a central repository to store data and builds the data models required at each stage from those developed in the previous stage.

2.5 THE ROLE OF METHODOLOGY

Often, the systematic collection of methods is gathered together into an overall framework known as a 'methodology'. Strictly, methodology is the study of method. However, in software terminology, the word has come to mean a systematic framework for software development defining a series of stages within the software development life cycle and methods within each stage to carry out the required tasks. Thus, within the software community, a more realistic definition might be:

'A methodology is a framework for the systematic organization of a collection of methods.'

These methodologies may be proprietary to a particular company, e.g. Information Engineering from Texas Instruments, Government sponsored, e.g. SSADM, or derived from academic study and within the public domain.

Tools to assist in software development, known as Computer Aided Software Engineering (CASE) tools, may be linked to a specific methodology, e.g. the Information Engineering Facility (IEF) CASE tool automates the Information Engineering Methodology (IEM), or may automate generic methods found in many methodologies.

Software engineering was introduced to try to formalize the development of software using ideas from other engineering disciplines. The idea that has been pre-eminent ever since is the idea of structuredness. The concept of structuredness is simply about breaking down a large problem which cannot be dealt with easily, into a series of smaller problems which can. The development of systematic procedures to produce structured code, which became known as 'methodologies', was the first widespread attempt to take account of quality issues during software development.

2.5.1 What is a methodology?

Lantz (1989) suggests that a methodology may be characterized by a number of features:

- *It can be taught.* A methodology involves a collection of methods. These may be ordered as a sequence of steps and the nature and order of each step may be taught.

- *It can be scheduled.* The time and resources required to complete each stage may be estimated and a project schedule drawn up accordingly.

- *It can be measured.* This schedule may be used to measure progress of the plan.

- *It can be compared.* The use of the methodology within a specific project may be compared with its use in another project, or with the use of another methodology.

- *It can be modified.* Methodologies can be improved in the light of experience. For example, SSADM (Structured Systems Analysis and Design Methodology) is now in its fourth incarnation since its adoption as a UK Government standard in 1981.

Methodologies may be developed for all or part of the software development process. Information systems development (ISD) methodologies such as IEM (Information Engineering Methodology) are concerned with the whole development process. SSADM is only directly applicable to the design and analysis phases of the process.

In order to see how a methodology is applied, consider a methodology for washing up. Washing up is a good application for a structured methodology as it is often carried out in a haphazard fashion.

A 'best practice' approach might be considered in 13 phases, described in Table 2.1 and illustrated in Fig. 2.5. This provides a rigorous and systematic approach to washing up. Once a clear procedure is in place, then we can put into operation a series of reviews for quality assurance. The process of washing up then becomes a systematic sequential process.

At each stage, monitoring and evaluation are required to check the effectiveness of the procedure. For example, in our washing up example, the state of the washing up water is a critical factor in the success of each stage. Therefore during each of the washing phases, ongoing monitoring is required. Similarly, the amount and effectiveness of detergent is another critical factor in the effectiveness of the overall process.

Where washing up and drying are carried out by two different people, this allows for a natural QA process to be incorporated, since the drier may reject items that are unsatisfactorily washed. However, the process should be designed to minimize the number of items failing to meet the required standard.

Table 2.1 Summary of washing up methodology

Procedure	*Description*
Sort Washing Up Into Categories	This process sorts the washing up to be done into categories of increasing dirtiness: glasses, cutlery, crockery, pots and pans used for cooking. This minimizes transfer of dirt and the need for changes of water. An inspection is required to ensure that all dishes are sorted correctly.
Clean Surfaces	In order to ensure clean dishes are not placed upon dirty surfaces leading to re-soiling, the surface on which clean dishes are to be placed should be inspected.
Rinse Dishes	The soiled dishes should be rinsed to remove excessive dirt. This should be subject to inspection, to ensure that it has been carried out to the required standard.
Wash Glasses	The glasses should be washed first, in order to ensure maximum cleanliness. All clean glasses should be inspected to ensure that they are cleaned satisfactorily.
Wash Cutlery	The cutlery should be washed next, in order to maximize cleanliness. All clean cutlery should be inspected to ensure that it has been cleaned satisfactorily.
Wash Crockery	After the cutlery, the crockery should be washed and inspected for cleanliness.
Wash Pots & Pans	Finally, the dirtiest items should be washed. After washing they should be inspected.
Dry Glasses, Dry Cutlery, Dry Crockery, Dry Pots & Pans	The drying should be carried out in the same order. Each phase is followed by an inspection.
Put Away Dishes	The clean dishes should all be put away and this should be checked.
Clean Up Sink Area & Bowl	Finally, the area used, the sink, draining boards and bowl should be washed down and inspected. A final report on the state in which the area has been left is required to complete the process.

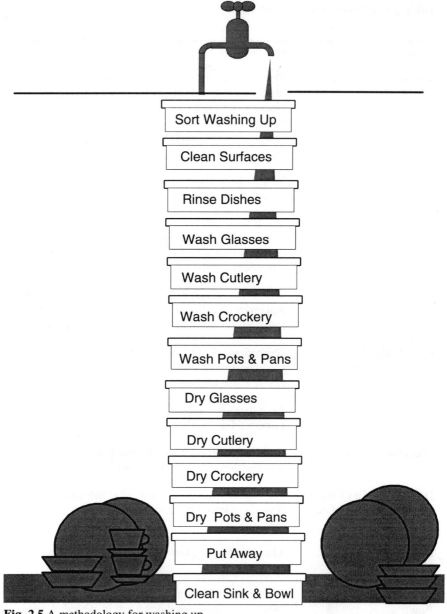

Fig. 2.5 A methodology for washing up.

A good methodology for software development has a number of characteristics:

- *Usability.* It should be easy to use and have good support provided by the vendor, since this is just as important to the long-term usability of the product.

- *Integrity.* A methodology should provide coverage of the whole life cycle to ensure integrity throughout the process.

- *Adaptability to local needs.* Methodologies are necessarily restrictive if they are to encourage good practice, but they should also be adaptable to the needs of a particular environment.

- *Clarity.* Documentation is a critical and often neglected area. Good documentation can be facilitated by the methodology and partly generated by associated tools. The methodology itself should be jargon-free and produce understandable output.

- *Automation.* Increasingly, methodologies are becoming automated through the use of tools. A good methodology should lend itself to automation.

The methodology is the basis for any CASE tool. Without a systematic and appropriate procedure, automation will not solve any of the software developers' problems.

2.6   THE ROLE OF CASE

Recent years have seen the advent of many software tools (Stobart, Thompson and Smith, 1991a) to support the software development process. Such tools are now given the generic name CASE (Computer Aided Software Engineering). The use of these tools can not only enhance productivity, by relieving the software engineer of some of the more tedious tasks in software development, but it will also ensure adherence to standards and, ultimately, increase quality.

Indeed, CASE tools have been promoted as one of the solutions that will counter the problems of poor software quality and inadequate documentation. The successful use of CASE should also enhance and improve software usability and maintainability.

CASE is the automation of existing software engineering methods and practices with the goal of improving both the quality of the product and the efficiency of the software developers. Such automation is new within the software engineering community; however, it has been applied for some time in fields such as computer-aided design (CAD) and computer-aided management (CAM), among others.

The automation of the software development life cycle requires the creation of a set of tools that will assist in the production of high quality software; ideally by automating every stage in the software development process. In practice, however, CASE tools provide varying levels of support throughout the software life cycle. That is, there is great diversity in tool functionality, design and in the user interfaces which CASE tools present to the software engineer. This situation has resulted in considerable confusion surrounding the true definition of what exactly constitutes a CASE tool.

CASE tools are now available to support and automate many stages of software development including:

- generation of structure charts;

- automatic generation of program code from a structure chart;

- automatic generation of documentation;

- consistency checks;

- screen design; and

- testing and debugging.

Those CASE tools that automate analysis and design techniques such as data flow diagramming, logical data structures and entity–relationship modelling are very different from those which automate the later stages of software production such as code generation by structure charts and the reuse of existing modules of code. Such differences have resulted in the definition of various categories of CASE tool, as summarized in Table 2.2 and Fig. 2.6:

Table 2.2 Types of CASE tool

Description	Also known as	Scope
upper-CASE tools	front end	automate the earlier analysis-based stages of the software life cycle
middle-CASE tools		automate the design-related stages of software production
lower-CASE tools	back end	focus upon actual code generation
integrated CASE tool		automate the complete life cycle

The Software Lifecycle

Requirements analysis	System & software design	Coding	Testing	Operation & maintenance

Integrated CASE tools (ICASE)

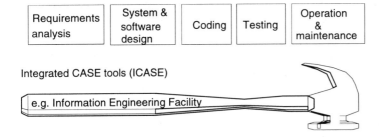

e.g. Information Engineering Facility

Upper/Lower CASE tools

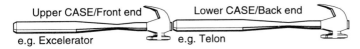

Upper CASE/Front end   Lower CASE/Back end

e.g. Excelerator   e.g. Telon

Upper/Middle/Lower CASE tools

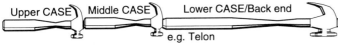

Upper CASE   Middle CASE   Lower CASE/Back end

e.g. Telon

Fig. 2.6 Types of CASE tool.

Thus, some tools facilitate analysis, some design and some both, whilst others are concerned with generating code. However, the latest generation of CASE tools are moving more and more towards the idea of the integrated CASE tool that attempts to automate (or at least offer support to) every stage of the software development life cycle. Some such tools (or sets of tools) are now emerging. However, the majority of current CASE technology focuses upon performing data consistency and conformance checks and automating the process of managing and documenting software production. This form of support enables software engineers to concentrate more on the creative design aspects of software fabrication.

Although there is currently little standardization in the CASE market, and the take-up of CASE technology in industry still remains somewhat low, it is still seen by many as an area of expansion for the future. The use of CASE tools may, at the very least, be expected to lead to increases in development productivity and the generation of quality software that conforms more closely to requirements.

Traditionally, CASE tools have focused around the data processing area, with a wide selection of CASE technology being available to help in the development of commercial software systems. In recent years, however, tools have become available for many other application areas.

This is also an area that is likely to grow and expand in the coming years.

2.7   SUMMARY

The main points of this chapter were:

- At a point in the historical development of computer systems, the degree of complexity made existing *ad hoc* methods unacceptable. This was known as the 'software crisis'.

- The proposed solution to the crisis was the application of engineering ideas from other disciplines to software development. This became known as 'software engineering'.

- The key ideas borrowed from engineering were establishment of clear goals, a clear plan, breaking down the overall problem into a set of simpler tasks, use of a systematic method to control and manage the project, use of suitable tools to support the process, evaluation and monitoring , testing.

- The resulting methods were known as 'structured methods' since they broke the problem down to smaller tasks.

- The process was known as the 'software life cycle' and the collection of methods required to carried it out became known as a 'methodology'.

- CASE tools have been designed to support and automate these 'methodologies'.

FURTHER READING

Sommerville, I. (1989) *Software Engineering*, 3rd edn, Addison-Wesley

This book provides a comprehensive treatment of software engineering. The references provided here refer to the 3rd edition, although a 4th edition has recently been published.

Constantine, L.L. and Yourdon, E. (1979) *Structured Design*, Prentice-Hall, New York.

Jackson, M.A. (1975) *Principles of Program Design*, Academic Press, London.

Jackson, M.A. (1983) *System Development,* Prentice-Hall, New York.

Yourdon, E. (1975) *Techniques of Program Structure and Design*, Prentice-Hall, New York.

Yourdon, E. (1981) *Modern Systems Analysis.* Prentice-Hall, New York.

These books are classic tests from the development of structured methods for the development of software.

Fisher, A. (1991) *CASE : Tools for Software Development,* Wiley, New York.

This text provides a gentle introduction to CASE tools combining details of specific methods and tools with a readable style.

Gillies, A.C. (1992) *Software Quality: Theory and management,* Chapman & Hall, London.

Chapters 6 and 10 discuss the relationship between CASE tools and software quality.

PART TWO

WHERE ARE WE NOW?

3

The DTI SOLUTIONS Programme (1989–91)

John A. Kirkham

3.1 INTRODUCTION

The SOLUTIONS programme was funded by the UK Department of Trade and Industry (DTI) to raise the awareness of the business community, particularly small to medium sized companies (SMEs), as to the benefits of using software engineering methods and Computer Aided Software Engineering (CASE) tools for developing Information Systems (IS). The core component in the programme's strategy was the promotion of 'best practices' derived from the experiences of other businesses. This was achieved by adopting a three-pronged strategy:

- media coverage to create awareness;

- quarterly newsletters and an audio-visual presentation to provide supporting information and ongoing commitment; and

- seminars and workshops to 'inform and educate' and to encourage action.

3.2 STRATEGY

The strategy identified two distinct target audiences and tailored its messages accordingly.

The first target was the 'purse-holder and decision maker' – senior managers whose influence and commitment would be needed to make an information technology (IT) project successful. These key messages were slanted to the business benefits of having a cost effective, properly developed IT plan.

The second target was the IT professional: those who had the responsibility for 'selling' IT internally and guaranteeing its credibility. The key message was not just technical excellence but also the vital importance of developing it as a profit-making component in the business plan.

Fifty events (seminars, breakfast meetings and technical workshops) were held throughout the country, attracting up to 100 participants on occasion. Some specialist events attracted even greater participation; for example, the sessions on real time systems and reverse engineering had 171 and 182 attendees respectively. The technical event for the IT professional was called 'Achievements with Software Engineering' and the management event was called 'IT for Competitive Advantage'. The technical event lasted from 11:00 to 15:30 hours and had a common introduction and conclusion between which three to four demonstrators, from a pool of twenty, gave presentations. The management event, called a breakfast seminar, lasted from 08:00 to 09:00 and was followed by a full English breakfast.

The format was a common introduction, an audio-visual presentation followed by conclusion and discussion. A demonstrator in the breakfast seminar usually presented in the technical event. The demonstrators talked not only about the advantages but also the problems they had experienced and how they had dealt with them. Other presentations were given by experts recruited from other initiatives being run by the DTI such as open systems and quality (TickIT).

The demonstrators played a crucial role in the success of the programme. They were found in one of three ways:

- The quickest and most effective way was through personal contacts. This enabled the programme to get off the ground quickly with people who were known and trusted. This provided about one third of the demonstrators.

- Vendors of methods and tools were contacted to see if they had any clients who would be willing to talk at an event. There were two methods of contact: a seminar was held in London, at which 40 vendors attended, and a letter was sent to any vendors who had not attended the London meeting (100 letters in all). This avenue provided another third of the demonstrators.

- The final approach was via the newsletter and those who attended the event. These people saw an opportunity to further the image of their company and themselves by speaking at SOLUTIONS events.

Once the contact had been made, one of the SOLUTIONS team was assigned to that potential demonstrator. The demonstrator either visited or discussions were conducted over the telephone and a two page summary produced. This was then discussed with other summaries at the monthly meeting with the DTI and suggestions made as to the content of the presentation. If the demonstrator was suitable, then they were added to the list.

Typically demonstrators were required who could relate their experiences to a wide spread of medium size enterprise using a variety of methods and tools. The type of software and hardware platforms was not important as the key was raising awareness rather than giving detailed technical advice. If the demonstrators satisfied these criteria and were thought to be good presenters, then they were accepted.

Some demonstrators were not suitable or found that their employers would not let them spend the time away from their work. The time spent on these was not wasted as their experiences appeared in the newsletter and on the audio tapes.

Once accepted, another discussion was held with the demonstrator to determine the structure and general thrust of the presentation. The presenter then prepared a first draft of the slides and supporting text. These were then reviewed until all parties were happy. A formal presentation was then held at Salford for two or three members of the SOLUTIONS team. A constructive critical discussion was then held to iron out any problems.

For the presentation it was felt that the critical factors were as follows.

- It should not be too technical, but rather aimed at senior managers stressing the business benefits. This message would also be relevant to the DP/IS managers who could use it as a lever to obtain the methods and tools to improve quality and productivity.

- The presentation must be interesting and stimulating.

- The presenter must be credible and professional.

- Slides must be simple and readable.

- The time for the presentation was critical, typically 30–35 minutes with 5-10 minutes for questions and discussion.

- The presentation should fit the underlying message of the SOLUTIONS programme.

The application of these procedures and criteria was reflected in the high quality of the resulting presentations.

At all the events a questionnaire was distributed and attendees were asked to fill it out before they left or post it from work. The aim of the questionnaire was to find out their opinions of the event and whether they would be investigating how they could use SE methods and CASE tools in the future.

Eight quarterly newsletters were published and each circulated to 5000 named business executives. Readers surveyed showed 70% of the recipients found the newsletter interesting, informative and relevant to their companies. A slide-tape presentation was produced as a visual guide to best practice in software development. At the end of the project a 'drive time' audio tape was produced, summarizing the key messages and case studies of the SOLUTIONS programme. Extensive media coverage, news items and feature articles were secured in national, local, trade and business media. Most of these were either based on case studies (Solomonides *et al.*, 1992) or dealt with the general proposition of the need for properly planned and managed software development.

The main achievements of the programme can be summarized as follows:

- Fifty management and technical events were completed;

- 2242 delegates representing 1867 companies attended;

- 77% of management seminar delegates were from SMEs, of which 47% were at director level and 32% line managers;

- 54% of technical workshop delegates were from SMEs, of which 12% were executives and 27% DP/IT managers;

- Over 80% were motivated to take action following the events;

- Eight newsletters were published and distributed to 5000 companies;

- Over two-thirds of the attendees distributed the information to other people in their company and over half investigated software engineering (SE) methods and CASE tools.

3.3   THE TAKE UP OF SE METHODS AND CASE TOOLS

In contractual terms the project was a success. We attained, and in many cases exceeded, the attendance targets set by the DTI. The analysis of the questionnaires after the events showed that most delegates felt the effort of attendance was worthwhile. However, the fundamental question is:

'Did the seminars manage to raise the delegates interest so that some action was initiated?'

A questionnaire was sent out six to nine months after the event took place. The purpose of the questionnaire was to decide, after the first flush of enthusiasm, whether the attendees' organizations had started to adopt SE methods and CASE tools. In other words had we raised their awareness to such an extent that they had investigated the use of SE methods and CASE tools in their organization. The choice of follow-up after six to nine months was purely pragmatic. It was felt that by this time the organizations would at least have started a study and may even have had the results and started implementation. Leaving the survey any longer increased the chances of the participants forgetting the SOLUTIONS event and meant that the DTI would not have the results of the feedback into their other programmes.

The questionnaire was individually addressed and printed on coloured paper to make it stand out against other printed material on the recipient's desk. As the questionnaires were returned they were logged. After approximately four weeks those who did not reply were sent another questionnaire. The first mailing produced most of the replies. Three hundred and forty replies were received for the attendees of the 'Achievements with Software Engineering' and 194 replies were received for the 'IT for Competitive Advantage' event.

3.4 ANALYSIS OF 'ACHIEVEMENTS WITH SOFTWARE ENGINEERING' EVENTS*

Not all the questions will be discussed; only the ones considered pertinent to the question, 'Did the organization do anything concerning SE methods and tools after the event?' In other words, was awareness raised to such an extent that the delegates initiated some action in their organization?

Rather surprisingly 45% of the organizations attending the event were already using SE methods. Perhaps they were coming to see what other people, the demonstrators and their competitors, were doing. We don't think that they misunderstood the reason for the event as delegates were generally satisfied with the event. After the event 50% of the delegates who had not previously used SE methods were persuaded to investigate such methods. They did this by obtaining further information from a variety of sources such as the National Computing Centre, supplier literature, training seminars and further research of an unspecified type. Some mentioned seeking management approval for finance, but nobody launched straight into use. Of those that did not do anything, 56% thought it not relevant, 21% their organization was too small and 23% the time was not ripe but may look at it later. The small organizations were usually consultants who were filling in gaps in their knowledge. They were also on the look out for clients and usually prefaced their question with 'I am John Jones, a consultant, and would like to ask the following question...'

Thirty-one per cent of the organizations were already using CASE tools. The reasons for this were similar to those for SE methods; they were coming to see what other people, the demonstrators and their competitors, were doing. Additionally, the definition of a CASE tool varied. Delegates argued that any tools that help produce systems are CASE tools such as project management tools, 4th generation languages or totally integrated CASE tools. One definition of CASE tools is:

'...software packages which automate or support one or more activities of the systems development cycle. They should have their own database holding the deliverables which they use and produce, and may optionally have a graphics front-end by which deliverables can be entered or updated manually.' (Rock Evans, 1990).

* see Kirkham and Stainton (1992) for further details

This definition would exclude project management tools but include 4th generation languages.

Table 3.1 shows the cross tabulation for the questions 'Were you at the time of the event using SE methods?' and 'After the event did you investigate CASE tools?'.

Table 3.1 Impact of events

	Were you at the time of the event using SE methods?		
After the event did you investigate CASE tools?	*Blank*	*No*	*Yes*
Blank	10	10	76
No	3	93	43
Yes	2	69	34

Table 3.2 Usage of tools and methods amongst attendees

	Were you at the time of the event using SE methods?		
Were you at the time of the event using CASE tools?	*Blank*	*No*	*Yes*
Blank	10	4	0
No	5	163	53
Yes	0	5	100

Of those already using SE methods at the time of the event 22% of them decided to investigate CASE tools to support the SE method. Perhaps they had already carried out the investigation of CASE tools appropriate for their adopted method before the event. On the other hand 40% who did not use an SE method investigated CASE tools.

A point stressed by many of the demonstrators was that a CASE tool could only be employed effectively if a suitable SE method is in place. A study by Price Waterhouse (1990) showed that one in five people using CASE tools had rejected them, leading to the term 'shelfware'. This is shown forcibly in Table 3.2 where only 3% are using an SE method with no supporting CASE tool. Of those using an SE method 65% supported the use with a CASE tool.

After the event, an encouraging 40% of those who had previously not used CASE tools were persuaded to investigate such tools. However, eleven claimed to have started to use a CASE tool. Of those that did not do anything, 19% were already familiar, 49% thought it not relevant, 8% had a change of role and many claimed that expense and time (24%) were prohibitive at this time.

3.5 ANALYSIS OF 'IT FOR COMPETITIVE ADVANTAGE' EVENTS

Figure 3.1 shows that the delegates' organizations were aware of the potential effect of IT upon competitiveness. Typically, two-thirds of the companies have an IT plan and in over 60% of them the IT and Business Plans were linked. This, if true, is a very encouraging trend as the Price Waterhouse IT Review (1992) cites the top issue as 'Integrating IT with Corporate Strategy' (see Fig. 3.2).

The delegates appeared to work for companies who took a long term view of the future. At the time of the event, 24% of the organizations were using SE methods and of the companies who had not previously used SE methods 53% were persuaded to investigate methods. 32% are now using SE methods. This represents an increase of 33% over the number at the time of the event. At the time of the event 20% of the organizations were using CASE tools and of the companies who had not previously used CASE tools, 36% were persuaded to investigate methods and 15% are now using CASE tools.

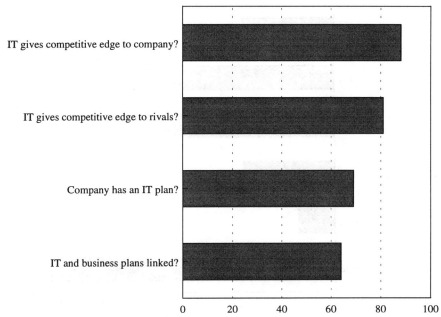

Fig. 3.1 Attendees' perception of impact of IT on business.

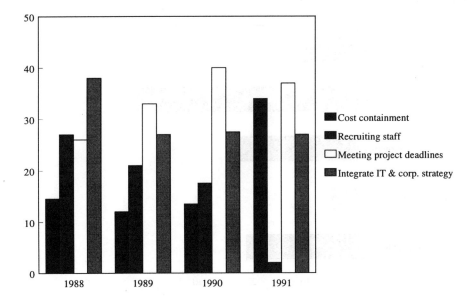

Fig. 3.2 The top four factors.

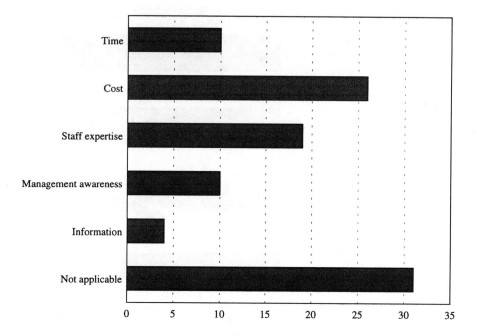

Fig. 3.3 Barriers against SE methods.

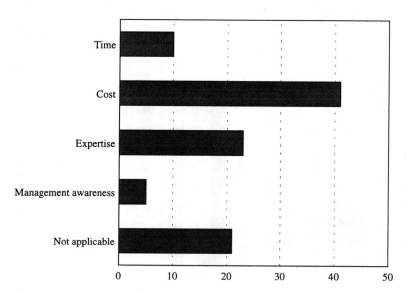

Fig. 3.4 Barriers to CASE tools.

According to the Price Waterhouse survey cited above, the IT departments' expenditure in the latter half of the 1980s has been restrained and cut back. Furthermore, the problem of cost containment has become one of the four key issues of the 1990s (see Fig. 3.2).

The main barriers against introducing SE methods and CASE tools into organizations are shown in Figs. 3.3 and 3.4. As can be seen in both cases, in descending rank order, the barriers to introducing SE methods and CASE tools are cost, expertise, time and management awareness. In an atmosphere of cost containment, cost, expertise and time become critical and companies are reluctant to increase costs and invest in new methods and tools.

3.6 CRITICAL SUCCESS FACTORS

It is worthwhile attempting to identify the critical success factors in the hope that this may help subsequent programmes of this nature. What was extremely rewarding was that SOLUTIONS not only succeeded in creating awareness, it also had impact; organizations who attended the events or received publications took action as a result. Delegates that attended the event felt that it was time well spent.

This was not a study of a problem or of 'what to do' and in that sense there are no conventional recommendations. Set out below are the factors that were important in helping the programme reach its objectives. It is for the reader to decide whether these factors are relevant in other programmes of this type and should be treated as recommendations. The following are the main factors:

- The project was approached as a marketing exercise; care was taken not to lose the prime objective of the programme which was to create an awareness of software engineering methods and CASE tools in British industry and encourage it to take action.

- Although the creation of quality events, newsletters and other delivery products, such as audio tapes and tape-slide presentations were important they were not the prime goal, but merely the vehicles.

- Driven by the above considerations the programme created, in a cost-effective manner, several deliverables that could be used flexibly to meet the customers' requirements.

- Central to the success of the programme was the ability to respond to feedback and be prepared to experiment with new ideas. This required close liaison with the DTI and the ability to back the proposals for change with relevant facts.

- The project required three very important skills, project management, technical expertise and public relations and marketing.

- Vital to the success of the programme was the quality and appeal of the chosen demonstrators coupled with the ability of the core team to provide a series of linking presentations to design effective events.

- Focusing on the business benefits was the most effective way to achieve the objectives of the programme.

- Careful choice of facilities and the geographical locations of the venue was very important.

- The quality of the mailing list database was important in attracting the right audience.

- Short events, such as Breakfast Seminars, were as effective in achieving the objectives of the programme as the longer events.

- The optimum number of delegates was around the 40 to 50 mark allowing for better audience participation than in the larger events.

- The programme also succeeded in getting organizations who were making use of SE methods to review their current practice. This was an unplanned achievement.

- Finally through Management (Breakfast) Seminars the programme was successful in targeting SMEs and green field sites, two of the main targets of the SOLUTIONS programme.

3.7 CONCLUSIONS

SOLUTIONS was a campaign to increase the awareness in British Industry of the existence and benefits of software engineering methods and CASE tools. The programme comfortably met and exceeded the contractual obligations regarding the number of events, average attendance and profile of people attending. It went substantially beyond these measures in providing a programme of events, newsletters and publicity that had an impact well above the norm for this type of programme. Both the technical and the managerial events were successful in raising the awareness of SE methods and CASE tools.

ACKNOWLEDGEMENTS:

1. This chapter was compiled after the SOLUTIONS contract which was carried out for the DTI from March 1989–March 1991.

2. The team consisted of Salford University Business Services Ltd, who provided the project management, the Information Technology Institute, University of Salford, who provided the technical expertise and PACE Communications Ltd who provided the PR and marketing.

3. Special mention must go to Paul Bowker (University of Huddersfield), Stewart MacKay (Salford University Business Services) and Mr Tim Ingham (PACE Communications) who contributed greatly to the success of the project.

4. The principal authors would like to thank John for this chapter and all the above mentioned for access to the material derived from the SOLUTIONS project.

FURTHER INFORMATION

Further information regarding SOLUTIONS is available from:
Stewart Mackay, Salford University Business Services Ltd,
Technology House, Lissadel Street, Salford, M6 6AJ.
Tel: 061 745 7457.

4

CASE usage in the UK, 1991*

4.1 THE UPTAKE OF CASE

Towards the end of 1990, staff at the University of Sunderland undertook a survey of the use of CASE within the United Kingdom (Stobart, Thompson and Smith, 1991b). The survey was undertaken by sending a postal questionnaire to 480 organizations involved in the development of commercial software.

The purpose of the survey was to quantify the actual usage of CASE in the UK. While many forecasts for the future and expected impact of CASE have been published, (Chikofsky and Rubenstein, 1988; PACTEL, 1985), few surveys had been undertaken to determine how much CASE is actually being used. Those surveys which had been completed (Hughes and Clark, 1990; Parkinson, 1990; Stobart, Thompson and Smith, 1990a) were either not UK-based or were undertaken before current CASE tools were available on the market.

There are many people around who will tell you that the level of usage of CASE is high; however, many of these are commercial CASE vendors and thus have a vested interest in making such statements and thus convincing potential CASE users that they, too, should invest in the new technology.

4.1.1 Objectives

The main objectives of the survey were:

* to determine the level of usage of CASE tools, particularly within the commercial sectors of computing in the UK;

---

* The authors gratefully acknowledge the contribution made by Simon Stobart and Barrie Thompson to the work in this chapter.

- to determine the hardware and software platforms used by those companies who had chosen to invest in CASE technology;

- to identify which areas of software development cause the most problems and how (if at all) CASE has helped to solve these problems;

- to determine those areas of the software life cycle which are currently automated, and to highlight areas which would benefit from automation in the form of future CASE tools;

- to determine the quality and efficiency benefits which have been achieved by companies who use CASE;

- to identify problems with current CASE technology and highlight areas for future improvement;

- to find out why many organizations have decided to reject CASE.

4.1.2 Results

The survey was sent to 480 organizations. The response rate was a relatively disappointing 25%, of which 23% of the whole proved to be useful responses. Follow up enquiries revealed that non-respondents had not responded because they did not use CASE.

The survey succeeded in painting a picture of an industry that has not yet really woken up to the use of CASE technology. That is, there appeared to be a relatively low (18%) usage of CASE among those people who replied to the survey (Table 4.1). The enquiries amongst non-responders suggested that the actual uptake was considerably lower since most people who did not reply did so because they were not using CASE.

There was, however, a great deal of interest in CASE and over half of the respondents indicated that they were either using CASE, going to use it or considering using it in the future. This promises a great deal more use of the technology as we move through the 1990s, particularly when you consider the new and much more advanced tools that are becoming available all the time. The major reasons given for rejecting CASE are summarized in Table 4.2 and illustrated in Fig 4.1.

Table 4.1 Uptake of CASE amongst respondents

Response	Percentage
Currently using CASE	18%
Currently evaluating CASE	26%
Considered but dismissed	13%
Willing to purchase	6%
Not evaluating	26%
Not sure	11%

Table 4.2 Reasons for rejecting CASE

Reason for rejecting CASE		Percentage
a)	cost of currently available tools	31%
b)	no management backing for CASE technology	16%
c)	current approaches appear to be satisfactory	13%
d)	lack of belief in the claimed productivity benefits	8%
e)	lack of supported methods	8%
f)	poor quality of tools	7%
g)	staff refusal	1%
h)	lack of belief in the claimed quality benefits	1%
i)	other	15%

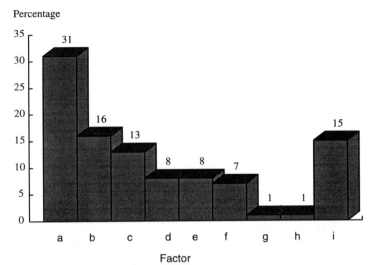

Fig 4.1 Reasons for rejecting CASE.

The respondents were gloomy about the future for CASE. Their perceptions of the future are given in Table 4.3.

Table 4.3 Perceived future for CASE

Perceived future for CASE	CASE users	Non-users
No future	16%	11%
Little improvement in tools	32%	46%
Substantial improvement leading to market acceptance	52%	36%
Become accepted by developers as preferred method	0%	5%
Totally change software development and maintenance	0%	1%

48% of respondents using CASE saw little or no future for CASE, whilst 57% of non-users were equally pessimistic. This degree of pessimism may be attributable to unrealistic expectations in the first place.

4.2 PROBLEMS AND DIFFICULTIES

The underlying reasons for the pessimistic view of the future of CASE tools was explored in three questions:

• Problems identified by current CASE users

• Required facilities for future tools from existing CASE users;

• Required facilities for future tools from those not currently using CASE tools.

The responses are shown in Figs. 4.2, 4.3 and 4.4 respectively. What emerges quite clearly is that those who have used CASE have different priorities from those who have not.

In particular, code generation and software testing facilities are a higher priority for non-CASE users and high quality graphics are less important.

Introducing CASE technology within a data processing department can, in itself, create a number of problems and difficulties (Stobart, Thompson and Smith, 1990b). If the department concerned already has a high commitment to the use of development methods, documentation, standards and quality assurance practices, the transition to a semi-automated approach using CASE can be quite straightforward. That is, because the organization is already used to working with methods and to providing documentation the introduction of CASE can simply be seen as supporting those procedures which already exist. This assumes, of course, that the CASE tools which are to be introduced within the organization support the methods which are currently in day-to-day use.

If, however, the CASE tools which are being introduced do not support current working practices because they conflict with the methods which are currently in use, there are sure to be problems as a whole new set of working practices will have to be introduced and learnt.

Similarly, if an attempt is made to introduce CASE technology within an organization which has not been used to employing software engineering methods, techniques and standards, there will certainly be a lot of very large problems. It is almost certainly better to introduce methods for software engineering gradually and to follow them with the tools to support the methods. Trying to introduce everything at the same time is probably a recipe for disaster.

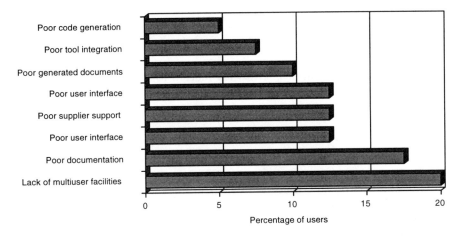

Fig 4.2 Major problems identified by existing users.

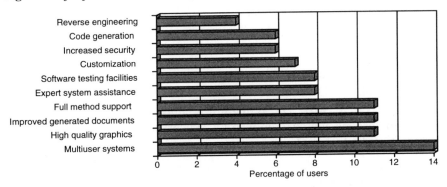

Fig 4.3 Required features identified by existing users.

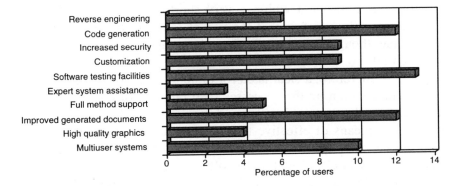

Fig 4.4 Required features identified by non-CASE users.

Typical problems that can arise when introducing CASE are:

- communication problems – how is team work supported by CASE?

- fear that introduction of CASE may lead to loss of jobs;

- training staff into the new way of working;

- productivity may not rise immediately – there will be a learning curve and a settling-in period;

- how can you be sure that the CASE product which you introduce will not be out-of-date in a few years?

- new hardware and software may be needed to run the new tools;

- the cost of buying CASE tools, hardware and training may be difficult to justify to management.

Of course, introducing CASE should bring benefits and advantages as well as problems. Otherwise it would not be worth even considering the introduction of CASE. The remaining chapters in this book will focus upon ten lessons which demonstrate successes, failures, problems and solutions and what can be learnt from these.

4.3 CONCLUSIONS

The area of CASE is, of course, dynamic and constantly changing, and any survey is only valid within a very short time scale. What can be clearly and safely stated is that the use of tools is still lower than one might have thought (or hoped); but the usage is growing and will continue to do so.

There is, therefore, a clear need for more information on tools and for clear documentation on the successes (and failures) of CASE usage. For CASE to be fully accepted within industry in general, there need to be much better means of effective technology transfer. In particular, there needs to be clear quantification of the benefits to be gained by the implementation of CASE within the software development process.

The UK Department of Trade and Industry (DTI) SOLUTIONS programme (SUBSL,1991) described in the previous chapter was set up to address many of these issues and particularly to raise awareness of best practice and experience in implementing both CASE tools and methods. Many of the case studies contained in this book are drawn from that programme. The aim of Part Three is to provide some of the required information, particularly in the areas of implementation and management of methods and tools.

4.4 SUMMARY

The main findings of the Sunderland survey described in this chapter were as follows:

- CASE was found to be used by a low proportion (only 18%) of respondents;

- Most CASE users are working with tools which are based on a microcomputer or a workstation (rather than a mainframe computer);

- Most CASE users are also applying a semi-formal software engineering methodology (e.g. Yourdon, JSD/P, SSADM);

- Those software developers who do not use CASE tend not to use any formal or semi-formal methodologies or techniques for software development;

- Several people indicated that future tools should provide better automated documentation, full method support, validation facilities and better code-generation;

- The ability to support team projects, multi-user development and computer aided co-operative working practices was highlighted as a major problem with current CASE technology;

- Less than 15% of respondents thought that CASE had no future at all, but nearly 50% were pessimistic about improvements in the near future;

- Most people thought that the use of CASE would increase in the future.

FURTHER READING

Stobart, S.C., Thompson, J.B. and Smith, P. (1991) The use, problems, benefits and future directions of CASE in the UK. *Information and Software Technology*, **33**(9) 629–636.

Full details of the survey and findings are presented in this journal article.

PART THREE

LESSONS FOR THE FUTURE

5

Methods come before tools

5.1 INTRODUCTION

This chapter focuses upon the role and importance of methods in the process of information systems development. In particular, lessons regarding the importance of methods are illustrated by two case studies. One of these is taken from the experiences of a large Government department, the other from a financial institution.

Both of these case studies illustrate the importance of methods and, what is more important, of clear commitment to those methods throughout the organization. Tools can, and do, of course, help; but without a method which everyone is committed to and adheres to, they are of little use or value.

The chapter begins with a brief history of methods, followed by a survey of some of the most important methods and tools. The two detailed case studies follow. A summary section presents the main lessons learnt and principles demonstrated by the case studies. The chapter closes with a list of reading material regarding methods and tools.

5.2 THE IMPORTANCE OF METHODS

5.2.1 Background

All branches of engineering have a set of methods and tools with which to work. For instance, civil engineers have methods to aid in the calculation of the stresses and strains on bridges, electronic engineers have methods to help in the lay-out of electronic components on a circuit board, and chemical engineers have methods based on chemical equations to help when working with chemical reactions. Information system engineering is no different to any other branch of engineering in this respect. Methods are equally important during the design and implementation of an information system as during the design and construction of any other engineering artefact.

Information systems engineering has developed from the discipline of software engineering which has, in turn, developed from the art of programming. It must not be forgotten that it is not that many years ago that there were no methods for the programmer to work with. Indeed, in the early days of computing, programming was truly an art and not a science. The early programmer had no methods to help him/her in the task of software construction.

Fig. 5.1 illustrates the way in which information systems development has matured over the years. It should, however, be stressed that information systems engineering is still a relatively immature discipline in comparison with many of the more established, and more traditional branches of engineering. Indeed, it is only in quite recent times that methods have become available for designing and constructing information systems. Even today, there are many methods around and little real agreement as to which is the 'best' method (if there can ever be said to be such a thing).

It was the so-called 'software crisis' of the late 1960s (Naur *et al.,* 1976) which brought a realization that methods were needed if software development was ever to become a truly professional engineering discipline. Out of this realization a series of methods were born. An overview of the history of information systems development methods is presented in Table 5.1.

Therefore, the information systems developer now has a set of methods with which to work. Which methods should one choose for a particular project? This is often a difficult question to answer as there may be many factors involved in making such a decision.

For instance, the following questions may determine the answer:

- What methods do I (and any other people involved) already know?

- What are the characteristics of the problem environment? Real-time? Data processing? Safety critical? etc.

- What tools do I have available to support the methods?

- Are any methods required by the client or because of legislation?

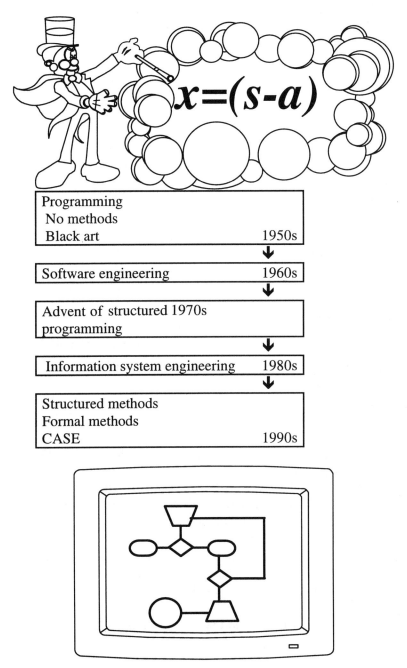

Fig. 5.1 A pictorial history of software development.

Table 5.1 A tabular history of methods

Period	Methods	Application
1950s	Flow charts	General purpose
1960s	MASCOT Structured programming	Real-time General purpose
1970s	JSP Yourdon Warnier-Orr	Commercial DP General purpose General purpose
1980s	SSADM JSD HOOD VDM, Z	Commercial Real-time Object-oriented systems Formal specification

The following section summarizes some of the most common methods that are available to the information system developer.

5.2.2 Categories of methods

Methods are now widely used throughout the software development community. A study of 230 organizations undertaken in the United Kingdom by market analyst Spikes Cavell in 1992 (Spikes Cavell, 1993) revealed that 73% of companies use one form of method or another. The survey also showed that almost 19% of those companies which were not currently using a method were planning to do so in the future. These results are illustrated in Fig. 5.2.

This represents, then, a major commitment to the use of methods within the UK information systems development·community. However, one common statement that is still made is:

'It doesn't matter what method you use, as long as you use a method.'

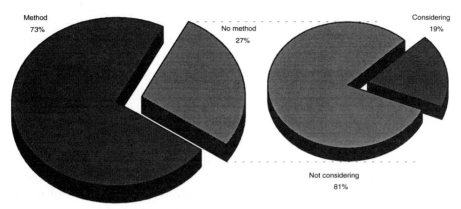

Fig. 5.2 Uptake of methods in the UK, 1992 (after Spikes Cavell).

There is certainly some truth in this statement but certain methods are better suited to certain application areas. For instance, methods such as SSADM (see below) are ideal for the development of large commercial systems, formal methods such as VDM (see below) are well suited to systems which particularly require mathematical rigour during their development to ensure high quality and reliability, and software design methods such as JSP (see below) provide a good approach to the development of commercial software modules.

A selection of the most common categories of methods is discussed below. Methods exist to address every aspect of information systems development including systems analysis, systems design, software module design, software implementation, validation and project management. The categorization given below is not, however, based upon the areas of the development life cycle which the method addresses. Rather, it is based upon the fundamental principles which underlie that particular class of method:

- Informal methods

- Data flow methods

- Data structure methods

- Structured techniques

- Formal methods.

Informal methods involve the application of the generic principles of software engineering such as structured programming and stepwise refinement. These are, however, basic principles and are not in themselves methods. There are, of course, many methods based upon these two principles, but simply applying these principles is a long way from using a method.

There are many software developers who will claim to use structured programming and/or stepwise refinement as a method. They are, no doubt, applying these important principles, but they are not really applying software development methods. The use of the term method implies the use of a systematic, standardized approach to software development. That is, the developer should follow a laid down set of rules which constitute the method.

There are, of course, many companies which have extremely respectable and useful in-house methods. Such methods may well grow out of a company's existing working practices. This will cause minimum disruption as the method will build upon practices with which the work-force are already familiar. There are also dangers in developing such in-house methods. They can lack the rigour and quality assurance rules that are built into external methods. The survey of Cavell found that a quarter of the organizations in the UK claimed to use an in-house method.

Data flow methods are based upon the flow of data though a software system. The method will usually result in the production of a data flow diagram of the software. This data flow diagram will then be refined into a program structure chart in terms of the three fundamental constructs: sequence, selection and iteration.

Program design methods that fall into this category are those developed by Constantine and Yourdon (Yourdon, 1989). System design methods which are based on data flow principles are Gane and Sarson's Structured Systems Analysis (Gane and Sarson, 1977), DeMarco's Structured Analysis and System Specification (DeMarco, 1979) and MASCOT (Modular Approach to Software Construction, Operation and Test) (Simpson, 1986).

Data structure methods are methods which attempt to model the structure of the data on which the software system is operating. The objective of this approach is to try to model the real world in terms of the data. Object oriented approaches can also be included in this category as they attempt to model the data on which the software system operates in terms of objects and the operations which can be performed on those objects.

Methods which fall into this category are those developed by Michael Jackson (1975,1983), namely JSP (Jackson Structured Programming) and JSD (Jackson System Development), and LCS (Logical Construction of Systems; Warnier, 1981).

Many of the more popular structured techniques have been formed from a collection of well-established procedures, rather than being based upon a basic principle such as data flow. Techniques which are often incorporated in such methods are:

- Structure charts

- Data flow diagrams

- Entity life histories

- Entity relationship diagrams

- Relational data analysis.

Methods of this type include SSADM (Structured Systems Analysis and Design Method; CCTA, 1990) and Information Engineering (Finkelstein, 1989).

SSADM is almost certainly the most widely used method in the UK. It was developed on behalf of the Government's Central Computer and Telecommunications Agency (CCTA) and is the mandatory method for any public service work in the UK. The method is now controlled by the BSI (British Standards Institute) and thus provides its large user base with a well-known, standardized and well-documented approach.

Although many people will argue strongly about the advantages to be gained from use of SSADM, there also some companies who would claim that it does not match their own particular requirements fully. For instance, one IT professional, whose company has customized SSADM to its own needs states (Spikes Cavell, 1993):

'There are very big holes in SSADM, which the manual is quite honest about. For example, if you look for guidance about what to include in a program specification, what they say is that you should produce a program specification to the standards of your organization and that's all.

Pure SSADM also gives you absolutely no guidance on planning the testing of a system beyond saying that at some stage you have to plan some testing. It gives no guidance about planning for the implementation, converting data from existing systems or constructing physical files.'

Methods such as STePS (Edwards, Thompson and Smith, 1994) have been proposed to help solve such problems.

All the methods which have been referred to above are semi-formal in nature. That is, they help the user to develop diagrammatic and textual models of the system and its data. Formal methods use mathematics to represent the system being modelled. The main argument for the use of formal methods is that mathematics is precise and unambiguous compared to other approaches which are more prone to both error and misinterpretation.

Methods which fall into this category are VDM and Z (Sommerville, 1989). Such methods are commonly used in areas where rigour and correctness are of prime importance such as safety critical systems.

However, no matter which method is chosen for a software development project the following important principles must be adhered to if the project is going to be successful:

- management must be committed to use of the method;

- staff must be fully trained in the method;

- formal review systems should be set up to ensure adherence to the method.

That is, starting off on a large development project, and using a formal or semi-formal method for that project, is not something that should be entered into lightly. It requires full commitment for all who are involved in the project. If that commitment is not present, then there are likely to be problems during the project.

The same set of principles can also be said to apply to tools. However, in the case of tools, it is even more important that there is a clear commitment to both the tools and the underlying methods. It cannot be stressed enough that tools are of no use without an underlying method. Tools are designed to support methods and, by definition, CASE tools are designed to support the software engineering process, which implies the use of methods.

5.2.3 Tool support for methods

A large number of CASE tools have been designed to support specific methods. A selection of these are shown in Table 5.2. Many other CASE tools are generic and support techniques which are common to many methods such as data flow diagrams, program structure charts and entity relationship models.

Table 5.2 A selection of methods and the supporting tools

Method	Developer	Tool
Information Engineering	James Martin Associates	IEF
		Excelerator
		Application Development Workbench
SSADM	LBMS/CCTA	LBMS tools
JSP	Michael Jackson	PDF Speedbuilder
Systems Thinking	Cognitus Systems Ltd	Ithink
Business Process Re-engineering (BPR)	TI	Business Design Facility (BDF)
DeMarco Method	Meta Systems	Structured Architect
Yourdon	Yourdon Ltd	Yourdon Tool Kit

However, whatever form a CASE tool takes, it will be used in conjunction with some sort of software development method. It is vital that the staff who are to use the tool are well-versed in the use of the method. This is a pre-requisite for the introduction of any CASE tools.

5.3 CASE STUDIES

5.3.1 Helping training centres work better

This case study focuses on the Information Systems Unit (ISU) of a UK Government department and how methods helped them successfully to run a training project.

Unlike most departmental ISUs, this unit was not restricted solely to IT projects. Responsibility was also present for some financial monitoring, typically of departmental running costs. The staff assignment section was also part of the services offered by the ISU. The ISU also had a section of specialist IT personnel and this section supported all aspects of IT within the department, ranging from mainframes through minis down to PCs, and developing software in conventional languages as well as in Fourth Generation Languages (4GLs). Standard packaged software was also supported by the ISU.

The department's IT strategy was influenced by their business strategy. This business strategy influenced everything done by the unit as well as the means by which it went about its business. Typically, there were four main areas that encompassed the entire strategy. These four areas were:

- communications

- hardware

- software

- methods.

It is, of course, the latter category that we are most interested in within this case study.

SSADM, PRINCE and business analysis have all been adopted, as well as some other, less formal, techniques. This case study illustrates how successful the use of these methods was, and how they were used to gain great benefits in the development project concerned.

The project in question was like most other projects developed in-house by the ISU, in that it did not solely relate to the ISU and the system users. That is, there were other parties who were interested in, and involved in, the system which was to be developed. Although the users had the major interest in the project, other groups were also involved.

- The data protection officer, who was responsible for registering the systems.

- The management team, who were involved in planning, resource training and general business issues.

- The Government department, which was interested to see how the system achieves its objectives, and how it might assist the department in achieving its overall aims.

- Central information systems development (ISD), as they were the owners of the technical staff, and had overall control regarding staffing levels.

- Trade unions, whose aim was to protect their members and to agree a suitable workplace agreement.

- Internal Audit, who may be the last on most people's list of interested parties but are, in fact, vital to the successful implementation of a system. In this particular instance, the ISU involved Internal Audit staff from the outset and reaped many benefits from such an arrangement.

The users of the system were spread throughout a large geographical area in Training Centres. There were 12 such centres, generally located on the outskirts of larger towns. Some of these centres acted as administration points for smaller 'satellite' units, of which there were five.

Other major users of the system were the Management Training Unit who wished to use the system to assist in administration, and the Headquarters branches, namely Administration and Finance. Their use would centre largely on query facilities.

The prime objective was to help the local managers become more autonomous and to take more responsibility for the generation of the data and use of the information produced. There were areas within the workplace where there was duplication of data and the system provided a means of reducing these phenomena. The hardware, software and communications installed provided the basic building blocks for the department's IT strategy.

The department had a staff training branch and a budget to cover training expenses. The department also supported staff development schemes such as the British Computer Society's Professional Development Scheme.

It was felt very strongly that if the system was to function efficiently then its users must be equipped to get the best from it. No outside consultants were required in the provision of training as the courses were designed, documented and taken by staff from within the department.

As part of the training project, systems were developed covering seven areas.

• Personnel records for trainees to monitor the educational achievements of trainees.

• Payroll interface to allow accurate and timely payment of trainees.

• Course diary details which correlate instructors and classes.

• Limited personal information on instructors including training history.

• Company records detailing those with links to the training centres.

• Records detailing applicants.

• Management information provided as requested and on an *ad hoc* basis

The benefits achieved already and those still to come were directly linked to the objectives of the project. As a tool in assisting local management to improve the accuracy and timeliness of its data, it was very successful in providing help in monitoring progress against pre-set management targets.

Duplication of data was reduced and a central focal point of information became available. The role of the marketing officer was greatly assisted by the capabilities of the system to identify trends and give information on recruitment and placement. Some direct financial savings were accrued (e.g. the reduced use of DataPost, improved accuracy leading to fewer payments being spoiled and so on).

Furthermore, as part of the IT strategy the group had become equipped to deal with even more widespread applications.

The project management method PRINCE was used to manage and control the project from the outset. The process was an iterative one, as illustrated in Fig. 5.3.

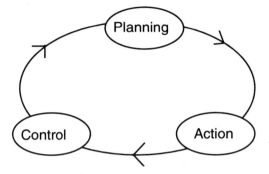

Fig. 5.3 Planning, action, control management cycle.

The questions that had to be addressed at the planning stage were:

- What are the objectives?

- What are the end-products?

- What activities are required?

- Have quality criteria been set?

- Where are the dependencies?

- Have control points been set?

- Do yardsticks exist by which to set time scales?

- What resources are required?

- What are the constraining factors?

The change control process must address the following issues:

- What is the change?

- What are the implications on the plans for the options?

- How critical is it that we do something?

- What is the best way forward?

- What are the consequences?

- Are there any knock-on effects?

- How is the business case affected?

The project board was the real managing agent of the project. It was manned by a chairperson and at least one senior user and one senior technical person. Their function was clearly defined and they assumed overall responsibility for the project.

It must be stressed that the members of this group were very senior members of the organization; this is vital for any project to be successful.

Training for board members is also vital so that they can appreciate the responsibility of their position. The project board should have the power to terminate the project if it becomes necessary at any point during the life of the development.

Another vital aspect of the PRINCE methodology is that of the project assurance team. Like the project board, the members must be chosen for their influence and skill in a particular area. There should be a user, and a business and a technical assurance co-ordinator, all of whose roles converge to give assurance on the approach and direction of the project. It needs to be stressed that they do not have any executive authority to take decisions, theirs is mainly an advisory role both to the project team and the project board. Some of their main functions include advising and assuring the stage team, assisting in the production of plans, assuring the project board, maintaining documentation and providing project continuity.

The approach described above was adhered to in this project, and was found to be very successful.

The Structured Systems Analysis and Design Methodology (SSADM) (Ashworth and Goodland, 1990) was used in this project. The most notable features of the use of SSADM in this project were the support tools used and the documentation produced:

- *Support tools.* There are various automated support tools available to support SSADM. In this project, Automate and Datamate from LBMS were used. These products have since undergone redesign by the suppliers and are now marketed as Automate Plus, a composite package of the earlier two.

- *Documentation.* In any project, particularly in a large one, the documentation produced and maintained is vital. SSADM produces much documentation but in a concise format that makes it easier for new members to join the team and become productive early.

The automated tool is invaluable in producing and cross-referencing the documentation. The screen and report layouts, generated with the method and quality assured with the PRINCE method, complement the documentation to give a total picture of the shape of things to come.

The method has many advantages but it should be stressed that it should not operate without a project management method controlling it and does not, in itself, guarantee success.

The main advantages found from using these tools and methods were:

- a staged approach;

- ease of use;

- the setting of attainable objectives;

- the use of Quickbuild (see below);

- the reduction of dependence upon development staff; and;

- the quality of documentation produced.

The decision had already been taken that the software would have to run in an ICL environment. This immediately restricted the implementation options. An evaluation exercise was carried out comparing two 4th Generation solutions (Quickbuild and Sygmar) with COBOL and a conventional file approach.

To complete the project within the given time scales effectively ruled out the possibility of using a conventional approach. Quickbuild uses a structured approach which eases learning and aids subsequent maintenance. Quickbuild was supported locally by ICL.

Immediately on completing the basic training course on Quickbuild, the programming staff were able to deliver programs. These may not have been the most efficient programs ever written but they indicated the short learning curve required.

Requirements for change to the existing system can more readily be put in place than if methods had not been using during system development. Experience in the language has increased the knowledge base of all the programming staff and this, coupled with the sharing of problems, has greatly improved the speed with which changes can be wrought. Again, the structure of the programs facilitates change and awareness of the database design enhances the efficiency of these new programs. Since the guidelines laid down in SSADM were followed throughout the project, it is safe to say that documentation is complete and to the required standard.

The project was judged a success. It was delivered within 5% tolerances on all three counts of budget, time scale and resource. The objectives, as detailed in the project initiation document, were met fully and the benefits have already been realized. The tools and methods used proved invaluable and the staff contribution to the project has been recently recognized by a round of promotions within the group.

5.3.2 A strong case for methods

This case study is based upon the experiences of a large financial institution. They have offices throughout the UK, assets of over £2 thousand million and several financial services subsidiaries, including an estate agency chain of 86 branches. Within the institution, the Business Systems Division comprises around 150 staff. The mainframes on which the vast majority of processing is done are BULL DPS7 machines and most systems have been built in-house using COBOL, which is still the main development tool.

In the first half of 1986, a merger increased the size of the organization by over 50% almost overnight. To cope with this, a major recruitment campaign was instigated in 1987 with the aim of doubling the systems development resource and bringing in systems project management skills from outside the organization.

Major development commitments precluded any changes in existing approaches until the second half of 1988 when two studies were initiated to consider improvements. The aim of the first study was to make recommendations on structured analysis and design techniques to be implemented within the institution, whilst the second was intended to investigate the CASE market place and to make recommendations as to the future potential for such tools in the company.

Several things quickly became apparent. The two projects described above could not be run independently of each other because they could result in incompatible recommendations. In particular, any CASE tools purchased would have to support the methods which were to be taken up.

Even if the above two projects were to be combined into one project, the objectives were not broad enough.

Two questions arose from the initial work carried out:

- Should the organization be selecting techniques without the framework of a good 'method' within which to use them?

- Should the study consider only CASE, or should other tools such as IPSEs (Integrated Project Support Environments) be included within its scope?

It was ultimately, and very sensibly, decided to run one project to look at methods, techniques and tools and recommend a way forward for IT within the company.

The project finally recommended the following:

- PRISM as a set of methods; and

- Maestro as a CASE tool.

PRISM was chosen because it offered a wide range of different but integrated methods. It allowed discrimination between major and minor projects and covered the areas of enhancement and maintenance. PRISM offered a logical separation of methods and techniques and did not tie the company to any specific suppliers of tools and methods. It also allowed them to maintain an existing, happy relationship with present suppliers in the area of skills training.

The Maestro tool was chosen because it was not restricted to specific techniques or methods, offering the flexibility to adapt to most techniques. A further useful feature was the help that it provided in the area of existing program maintenance.

The methods for business study, systems development, enhancement and maintenance and personal systems development were purchased. They were used in conjunction with the handbooks provided for quality management, project management, risk management, structured techniques and the information centre.

At the time of writing, the company had successfully implemented the business study method. This involved integrating the method into their procedures, producing standards for all the deliverables and extra guidelines where the method was not clear, running pilot projects, learning and applying lessons, and running a one-day introductory seminar for all systems development staff. This was not an easy process.

A methods steering group was established to direct future implementations. The lessons learnt were applied in the rest of the implementation, including some of the following principles:

- The users of the methods should be treated as customers. They should be involved in the processes of design and implementation and educated properly.

- Similarly, the end users should be educated about the methods, especially concerning their involvement and commitment as a critical success factor.

- The IT staff require a usable, practical method. The IT customers should see obvious business benefits resulting from application of the method.

- Commitment must be shown to the methods and techniques and the quality which follows from them.

- The methods should be fully adopted by the organization, and full commitment should be given to these methods. Even where they are bought off the shelf and implemented unmodified, they should be wrapped up in the company or departmental logo, so that they become 'their own'.

The methods must also be 'sold' to senior management outside IT, concentrating on business benefits, and not the details and 'bells and whistles' which you obtain when you adopt the methods. If they do not accept the method, it is unlikely to be a successful implementation.

A large number of the problems with IT projects had stemmed from failure to concentrate on the initial stages of the project life cycle. Implementing the business study, which comprises a business-based problem definition and feasibility study, has addressed this issue. More specifically, it means that business problems, not technical solutions, are what now drive IT projects. Furthermore, measurable, quantifiable project objectives are set, based on the business problems and requirements. Communication across departmental boundaries is improved. The result is healthy arguments about objectives and justifications before the development, rather than after implementation.

Finally, projects which should not go ahead are stopped by data driven management decisions, not crippling overruns and failure to achieve invented benefits.

A proposal for the purchase of the Maestro CASE tool was put to the company's executive once some experience of using the PRISM method had been gained. It was rejected because they were not satisfied with the lack of a convincing financial justification for an expenditure of £1 million over 5 years. At the time, the rejection was painful and seemed short-sighted, but with hindsight it is hard to argue with.

The company decided to carry out a formal business study into the area of CASE/IPSE tools. The reason for this is not so much a retreat from the initial selection as a recognition that it was 18 months since the selection was made and the market place had moved on. During that time, much has been learnt about the methods and techniques which the tool would be automating and the business study method has proved useful

5.4 SUMMARY

This chapter has focused on the subject, and importance, of methods. Methods are at the very core of the software development process. Without methods there is no structure, no standardization, little documentation and less opportunity for formal review approaches. Methods help add rigour, formality and hence should ensure a higher quality end-product.

Tools can also be of great benefit and can also add to the quality of the end-product. However, tools are of no use on their own. They must be accompanied by methods. Indeed, the tools are only there to support the method. Tools can help the software engineer work more efficiently and more accurately but they cannot make up for the lack of a methodical approach to software development.

The most important points to be remembered from this chapter are:

- A need to concentrate on business issues; these are the most important part of any major project or development.

- The IT section has learnt that to implement a new method or technique, they have to sell it hard and do it efficiently and effectively.

- It is important to educate and involve everybody.

- A real management commitment to quality is needed.

- A good project management culture is vital to the success of any large project.

- Good communications and co-operation between all departments are the key to success.

- A stable environment with a meaningful IT strategy is of prime importance.

Finally, two general principles emerged from the work:

- First, methods must come before techniques which must come before tools; and

- the more that you need methods, the harder they are to implement, and vice versa.

FURTHER READING

Ashworth, C. and Goodland, M. (1990) *SSADM : A Practical Approach*, McGraw-Hill, London.

Of all the software methods available in the UK, the adoption of SSADM by the UK Government makes SSADM arguably the most significant. This text provides an excellent introduction to the method.

Barker, R. (1990) *CASE Method: Tasks and Deliverables*, Addison-Wesley, Wokingham.

This book is tied to ORACLE's proprietary CASE method but gives a good insight into a typical method of this type and thus complements the SSADM text.

6

Evolutionary not revolutionary change

6.1 INTRODUCTION

This chapter discusses the problems and pitfalls of introducing new technology into an organization. In particular, it focuses upon the problems which can arise when introducing CASE tools and the methods and approaches which accompany them into a new environment.

The chapter begins with a discussion of the problems of change, and how to manage these, followed by two case studies. The chapter concludes with a summary of the lessons learnt from these two case studies, and some pointers towards the important factors to be taken into account when introducing change into any organization.

6.2 MANAGEMENT OF CHANGE

6.2.1 Dealing with change

Introducing new technology into any organization can often lead to problems and difficulties. The organization concerned will already have its own set of procedures, working practices, methods and ways of doing things. There will be staff in the company who have been trained in particular ways of working and may, therefore, resist changing to any new ideas and the use of new technology. There may be existing equipment which is to be replaced and superseded by the new technology; these may be computers or other new types of hardware.

Whatever the reasons, there will nearly always be a reluctance to any form of change. The greater the change, the greater will be the resistance. This, of course, is human nature to some extent. This can be illustrated by a simple example.

Consider that you are safe at home indoors in your lounge. You are sitting by the fire watching the television. You are warm, comfortable, secure and contented. You are wearing light clothes and your carpet slippers. Your lounge is at a warm, steady temperature. You are in an environment with which you are familiar and you have nothing to fear or worry about.

Suddenly you are transported to an Arctic wasteland. You are surrounded by nothing but the bleakness of white snow. A blizzard howls around your head. You still wear only your light clothing. You are lost, freezing and terrified but you know that you must do your best to cope within this new environment. You will search for shelter and try, as best you can, to find a way to keep warm. This is a basic human instinct; we will always try to find a way to protect ourselves and to survive (if, of course, survival is possible in such a bleak scenario!).

Fig. 6.1 Extreme example of revolutionary change.

This is a (rather extreme) example of revolutionary change. The individual in this nightmare scenario has been transported to a totally different and alien environment and left to cope as best he/she can. You will, of course, think that such an example is too extreme and that such change situations can never happen. That is true; but the equivalent change situations in terms of work environments can be surprisingly commonplace. That is, quite large and severe changes are often put into place quite quickly with little thought for the consequences to the organization and the individuals who work within it.

Such extreme change is, without a doubt, a recipe for disaster. Let us reconsider the above scenario, but this time take an evolutionary approach to the change.

You are again safe at home indoors in your lounge. Once again you are sitting by the fire watching the television. This time the telephone rings. You answer the telephone and hear the voice of your boss, who invites you to his office the next morning to discuss an important assignment for the magazine for which you write.

The next morning you arrive early at the office. Your boss is waiting for you and he invites you into his office. He shakes your hand, makes sure that you are comfortable and asks his secretary to give you a cup of coffee. 'Now, Desmond' he begins. 'I have a very important assignment for you. It is very important to the company but it is also very different to what you are used to and might, at first, seem a little strange. However, I hope that you will hear me out and then you will realise why I feel that you should do it.'

He continues, 'I need someone to write a piece on the conditions in the Arctic. It is something that we've tried to cover before but we've never really succeeded because none of our writers have really experienced the climate and the situation there. To remedy this we'd like to send you to the Arctic to get the inside story on what it's really like to be there.'

At first this seems a crazy but intriguing idea. You are quite concerned about how this assignment will work out. Your boss assures you that you will undergo a full training programme before making the trip to the Arctic. You will be supplied with all the necessary clothing and equipment. You will be given some simulated experience of cold climates before you go there. You will undergo thorough medical examinations before you start out. You will be trained in survival techniques and so on. Your boss has really thought this through beforehand and tried to cover everything.

However, he finishes by adding, 'I feel that it is important that we also consider carefully your views and feelings in such an important, and new, assignment. So have a good think about it, and let me know if there is anything that you feel I've missed and any other ways that we can prepare you for the project. For it to work well, we need your full commitment, interest and enthusiasm. I'd like us to work closely together on this one.'

So, in this scenario, when you are arrive in the Arctic wasteland, you are prepared. You have undergone training, you have covered everything properly before making the change. The acclimatization programme which you have undergone has ensured that the climatic change is, to some extent, gradual, and does not come as an extreme shock to your system. The change has been engineered in an evolutionary manner, rather than a revolutionary manner.

Although the above example is somewhat extreme and unlikely, it does illustrate a number of important points:

- Change should be made in an evolutionary, iterative and gradual manner.

- Revolutionary change is a recipe for disaster.

- If the objectives of the change are explained carefully to staff, and they can see the benefits to be gained, they are more likely to accept it.

- If you can gain staff commitment to change, that change is more likely to succeed.

- People factors are the most important in any change scenario.

The last point is very important. If any organization needs to make major changes they must get the people in that organization on their side. This will involve:

- Staff training. A full training programme should be put into place so that all staff are prepared for the impact of the change.

- Negotiation with trade unions may be necessary. This is particularly true where retraining or redundancy is planned.

- Redesign of all procedures, manuals and systems connected with the change.

Fig. 6.2 illustrates the difference between revolutionary and evolutionary change. Revolutionary change is a sudden step change which takes a system from one state into another. The results of such a sudden change are:

- severe shock to the system;

- staff dissatisfaction, discontent and dismay;

- high cost of investment in capital equipment;

- problems and perhaps even failure!

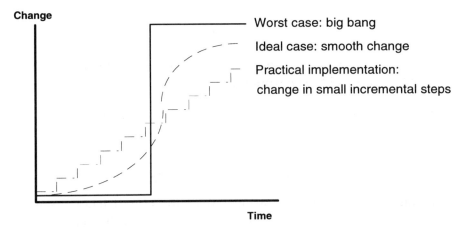

Fig. 6.2 Evolutionary and revolutionary change.

The staff of any organization are the vital resource and their insecurity in the face of revolutionary change may well be enough to prevent its success. Even if the staff are able to be convinced, the 'big bang' approach does not allow for effective evaluation of each stage, and thus no lessons may be learnt from each step before the next is taken.

It is almost inevitable that a step change will require a large capital investment. It is difficult to predict the effectiveness of that investment when so many factors are changing at once, any one of which could affect the effectiveness of the investment. From a management perspective, revolutionary change represents an uncontrolled step, which cannot be realistically planned and managed.

The only case where such a step might be justified might be in an organization where traditional values and practices were so entrenched that only a violent shake-up could affect change. If this approach is adopted, then a period of great uncertainty and trauma must be accepted as an inevitable consequence.

Gilb (1988) records a graphic example of what can happen when a big bang approach is adopted, in the context of introducing a global MIS, known as the corporate information system, into a large motor manufacturer.

Work had been running on the CIS for five years. It had a budget of eighty work years.

The company had attempted to manage the project effectively. They had:

• consulted the business management literature;

• carried out a feasibility study using external consultants for two calendar years and fifteen work years;

• bought in the biggest and latest computer hardware and software;

• used structured methods for the project;

• paid up when the project ran over budget initially.

In spite of this, after five calendar years the project had consumed twice its allocated eighty work years and was not contributing anything useful. Worse, it was possible to show that the system would never be able to handle the quantity of work required of it. To process the required number of transactions in a day, the system would have to complete each transaction in seconds. In practice, many transactions were taking minutes.

The size and complexity of the system simply could not be swallowed in a single chunk. Although this example is not concerned with the introduction of CASE methods and tools, the same principles apply.

Fig. 6.2 also shows evolutionary change. In its ideal form, it is a smooth, gradual process. In practice, it is likely that a practical realization would consist of a series of small, iterative stages. Either way, both the staff and the organization are eased into the changes in a much more sensible and human manner. The results of the evolutionary approach are:

• staff commitment to the process (if it is explained correctly);

• gradual spreading out of cost over time;

• staff satisfaction;

• success!

The evolutionary approach allows staff to adjust gradually to new ideas. It also allows expenditure to be spread over a period. Above all, it allows for proper planning beforehand and evaluation afterwards to allow adjustment of the overall process.

The management of change is a subject in its own right with excellent texts provided by Peters (1982, 1988) and Stacey (1990) amongst others. These texts will provide detailed approaches to the management of change. However, before a detailed approach to the management of change can be adopted, there must be a recognition that the process requires managing, and that change cannot simply be allowed to happen in a random and destructive way. Many organizations only learn this the hard way by experiencing the consequences of unmanaged and unmanageable change.

Kliem and Ludin (1992) focus upon the 'people' side of change management and stress the importance of preparing staff for any changes which are to take place in their working environment. Failure to do so, they warn, will result in resistance which may display itself as:

- high staff turnover;

- high absenteeism rate;

- sabotaging change; or

- ignoring change and finding other ways of doing things.

They identify three distinct groups in any change scenario:

- the change target, who are the group of people whose working practices are to undergo change.

- the change sponsor, who provides the resources to effect the change.

- the change agent, who implement the change.

Without question, the people are the most important factor to consider when implementing any change scenario within an organization. The importance of people is discussed further within the next chapter of this text.

6.2.2 CASE technology

Introduction of CASE technology is no different to the introduction of any other form of new technology. The arrival of CASE will be a significant change, which will bring with it a new set of challenges and problems. Such problems may include:

- fear of redundancy amongst staff;

- the need for adequate training;

- short term productivity losses;

- loss of investment due to obsolescence;

- the need for new hardware and software;

- justification to management.

There is a natural fear amongst staff that introduction of CASE may lead to loss of jobs. Staff may feel that computerizing the software engineering process will mean that the organization will need fewer software engineers. The claims made by vendors about productivity may fuel this fear. However, this is not the case. It should be made clear to staff that the introduction of CASE will enable them to work in a more productive and efficient manner, and will enable them to produce higher quality software systems.

Training staff into the new way of working is essential. CASE tools need to be learnt, as do the methods that go with the tools. Chapter 2 has discussed how methods should come before tools. This is an important part of the evolutionary change process.

Productivity may not rise immediately. There will be a learning curve and a settling-in period. This should be expected and planned for. The long term benefits should prove to outweigh considerably any losses which are incurred in the short term or any investments in time which are necessary to get the new CASE tools to work properly (and be used effectively).

How can you be sure that the CASE product which you introduce will not be out-of-date in a few years, and more change will be needed? This is, of course, a real worry with the introduction of any new technology. All that one can do is be careful and take your time when choosing a set of CASE products.

New hardware and software may be needed to run the new tools. This will, in itself, require further change. This must also be planned and budgeted for.

The cost of buying CASE tools, hardware and training may be difficult to justify to management. That is, justifying the need for, and in particular the cost of, change may be difficult. The long term benefits of the introduction of such tools need to be stressed. Unfortunately, the lack of many clear, quantified success stories often makes this a difficult part of the process.

The problem of change concerning CASE is that we may ask staff to adapt not only to large amounts of change but different types of change. Staff may be asked to swallow change in software development methods, tools, documentation, planning, estimation, management and team working.

This degree of change may well prove impossible. Even where the change is possible, keeping track of it in order to manage and guide that change may still be impossible

Of course, introducing CASE should bring benefits and advantages as well as problems; otherwise it would not be worth even considering the introduction of CASE. The next section of this chapter describes two success stories. These successes have been a direct result of an evolutionary, as opposed to a revolutionary approach.

6.3 CASE STUDIES

6.3.1 Making it work in the end

This case study focuses on a manufacturing company which makes and prints high quality cartons for the food industry. The company uses a range of high technology equipment to print, cut, crease and glue the cartons. The company employs 150 people and has a turnover of £10M.

The company employed a local software house to write a system for sales order processing, estimating, stock control, etc. This system was specified in quite an *ad hoc* manner in traditional 'back of an envelope' manner and written in BASIC to run on a minicomputer. Perhaps unsurprisingly, the system did not quite match up to the expectations of the company and certainly did not match all of their requirements.

For instance, the software did not cater for record locking and yet the system was intended to be multi-user. The system never worked and was very unreliable. Consequently *ad hoc* parallel manual systems were developed by the company to cover the deficiencies of the system.

This rather ramshackle computerized and manual system was inherited by the commercial manager. The senior management in the company were not convinced that computers were of value to the company (perhaps not surprisingly, given their previous experience). They were, therefore, not keen to invest any more in computer systems. The commercial manager, however, was convinced of the value of computer systems. He became the 'user champion' and got permission from the board to go ahead with a new computer system. They were fully supportive once the decision to go ahead was made. On the basis of their experiences a 'softly, softly' approach was adopted.

A grant was obtained from the Department of Trade and Industry and a complete analysis of the requirements of the company was carried out and documented. This requirements document contained a detailed description of all the business processes in terms of data flow diagrams and entity-relationship models along with examples of all documents used in the manual system.

This requirements document was sent out to a variety of firms, to enable them to put forward tenders for production of the system. Many put forward off-the-shelf systems but on being asked to do detailed demonstrations withdrew. Some firms submitted bespoke systems. One of these actually employed personnel from the previous company as contract programmers.

None of these firms were considered suitable by the company. The consultant who had written the requirements specification was invited to tender on the condition that maintenance support could be found. This was arranged by buying accounts and payroll packages from a minicomputer vendor who agreed.

The system was developed on an IBM PC using an applications code generator. Using the requirements specification as a base, a prototype system was developed. The prototype programs, screens and reports were validated by the users in paper form. This was a very important part of the development process. The company realized the mistakes it had made previously and was determined not to make them again. Once the 'paper model' had been agreed, the code was generated and the system was tested by the users. This cycle was then repeated until all the users were satisfied with the system. Parallel with the development, negotiations were carried out and a minicomputer purchased.

The COBOL code was ported over to the target machine, and then compiled and tested. Because of the integrated nature of the system it was decided to go 'live' on all the system, some 100 programs, simultaneously. There was really no choice as the old system was continually breaking down, had duplicate data and lost records, leading to very low company morale concerning computing systems. The system successfully went 'live' with very few problems and is now the cornerstone of the company's operations.

The system was designed for a company of £6M turnover. It went live a year ago when company turnover was £8M and is still running this year with a company turnover of £10M. The hardware has been upgraded and now supports some 20 terminals and four printers. Users are actively demanding further functionality as they realize the potential of the computer system. The system is independent of any hardware supplier. The system cost £100 000 for both hardware and software and took about a year to develop and implement.

It is used by the commercial manager and his staff who are able to provide up-to-date information to their customers. The system is also used on the shop floor and there is a constant dialogue with the office staff to ensure that orders are met on time. The factory works on a two shift system because of the volume of work. The system also provides a wide variety of management reports on raw material stocks (50% of cost of product), finished goods, machine utilization, etc. The management believes that in the long term this will enable them to manage the company much more efficiently and effectively.

The company had a bad initial experience of IT, but it has learnt from its mistakes. The lessons learnt have ensured that a successful system was developed 'second time around'.

6.3.2 An evolutionary engineering approach to developing business systems

This case study concerns a company within the textile industry. In the late 1970s and 1980s, the company was in deep recession. However, in more recent times the company had achieved considerable improvements due to the successful implementation of a recovery plan.

The nature of the group is diverse and covers many sectors of the textile industry. This leads to a demand for information systems to reflect the diversity of processes, size and methods of control for the companies in the group.

In 1984, the group attempted to meet the demand for systems in the conventional manner of preparing a definition of requirements and selecting packaged software to meet these requirements. Unfortunately, this project both failed to produce benefits and to meet expectations of time scale and cost. In view of this traumatic experience, the board commissioned a team of consultants to assist the information systems department in a strategy review.

The diversity of a large de-centralized textile group posed a significant challenge for information technology. Following a detailed review of the experience of the group, the principles for the development of an information technology strategy were defined as:

- to provide systems suitable for each industry sector and size of company;

- to consider the adoption of packages, where applicable;

- to control IT costs through a policy of standard hardware, operating system and development methods.

A review of alternative strategies was conducted against these principles. It became apparent that the route of implementing packages (either single or multiple) was impractical. The alternative of allowing each operating unit to select their systems was too expensive in capital and revenue terms, and the development of bespoke systems using conventional languages could not meet realistic targets for cost and time scale.

Attention was therefore turned to the use of 4GLs and, in particular, the Progress Software Corporation's PROGRESS Language. This was chosen for its productivity, facilities robustness, reliability, operational features, portability and cost and because it provided a single integrated environment for the whole application.

The potential drawback was that there was little practical experience and support within the UK, and consequently there were attendant risks of relatively unproven performance in the field. It was felt, therefore, that the feasibility of the method should be established with a pilot project.

A specification was prepared for a stock control and material traceability system. A clear definition of the objectives, milestones and project control methods was established prior to commencement. These objectives were used to prove the performance claims of PROGRESS both in development and operation of a system.

An objective of a 50% reduction in development time was set and the programming effort using conventional languages was estimated. The time spent on every activity was recorded against the estimate and all objectives were met, with many being improved upon dramatically. In addition a number of other benefits in terms of ability to prototype, robustness, user friendliness and ease of future enhancement and maintenance became apparent. These would result in greater cost savings in the future. The capability of the 4GL to be used for prototyping was impressive and had clear benefits in guiding inexperienced users to definitions of their requirements.

The objective of the project was to produce fully integrated business systems for the decentralized operating companies in the group. It was considered that certain key elements were required by all companies and a specification was raised against this. This 'core' system was developed using the 4GL and used as a prototype to demonstrate to the companies in the group. Various packages written in PROGRESS were integrated with the core system. The demonstration of the prototype was used to assist users in producing a formal definition of their requirements. The conventional process of producing operating procedures, staff training, data capture and pilot running was followed leading to the implementation of the system.

For each industry sector a 'major' site was nominated at which extensive analysis was undertaken. A 'reference' site was used for each sector to check the findings from the major site. It was recognized that for the pilot project that there was a need to introduce a methodology and Structured Systems Analysis and Design Methodology (SSADM) was selected. However, the belated introduction of a methodology initially slowed project progress. A more significant delay was caused by problems of recruitment and a training scheme was introduced.

Each company was requested to form a working party which provided the forum for discussion of the findings and initial design specifications and a method of communicating with end users. A Business Systems Definition (BSD) was produced using techniques from within SSADM and was 'indexed' by a Problem/Requirement list which identified where and how a solution was proposed. At this stage, the working party was requested to agree that data and functionality were correct in principle.

Following this agreement in principle, the normalization techniques of SSADM were used to produce the Database Schema, on which an independent review was carried out, from which it was concluded that the database was an efficient base on which to work. Programming of the core, despite the systems complexity and other daily commitments, exceeded the target set and project slippage was reduced. Programming of the major programs was also carried out at this time and system testing undertaken in parallel with this programming.

Working parties from all 12 companies in the group were given presentations of the system, which were followed up by workshops where end users and their managers were requested to use their own data and as many problem scenarios as they could envisage. Despite higher levels of work than anticipated there was a lower level of enhancement and milestones continued to be met.

At this stage, two representative sites were chosen for the initial 'pilot' running and testing of the database and programs. This process led to no functional or data changes but some enhancements were necessary to improve user friendliness. This was followed by 'live' operation at the two representative sites while at the same time 'pilot' operation was underway at two other companies within the group in preparation for 'live' operation. Implementation of the remaining companies was planned at the rate of two per quarter.

Targets were set in two major areas to assess the success of the project. These were considered to be the improvements in time scale, cost and quality of the systems produced and the resultant improvements in performance of the operating companies. A number of objectives were set by the operating companies for the purposes of monitoring the success of the project and each site set a monetary value on these savings to enable performance to be measured.

Within a diverse group the adoption of these methods allowed modern, effective information systems to be more readily accepted and used by staff in the operating units.

The use of a fourth generation language, in this case PROGRESS, brought a number of advantages. A simple 4GL language could have been used to offer the same facilities on UNIX and MSDOS based machines. Improvements in productivity during the coding phase were estimated to be at least 50% for 'complicated' programs and far greater for simple enquiries and reports. However, some of these improvements tended to be traded off against producing systems of higher quality.

Hence, future maintenance and enhancement were simplified and system testing was found to be quicker.

There were benefits in the area of staffing, too. Training of new staff without 4GL experience was found to be speedier. A staff structure based on Analyst/Programmers, rather than segregation of the two disciplines, proved to be more effective with the introduction of a fourth generation language and resulted in a smaller department.

The use of prototyping and piloting was very valuable. The combination of these approaches improved communication and understanding of the system.

A cost effective, cohesive and rational approach was taken to development methodologies, operating systems, hardware and applications resulting in cost savings. Effective systems were provided at a cost equivalent to 3.5% of turnover. These systems required just 10 staff to service all 12 companies. The resulting lower cost systems allowed IT to be applied to operating units where it would otherwise be uneconomic.

However, a number of lessons have been learnt from the experience:

- The company found that it was essential to have a good analysis and design methodology, otherwise it is difficult to move from the prototype to the production model. A CASE tool should be considered to support the methodology.

- As a result of their experiences, the company felt that prototyping must be used with caution. A balance must be struck between the benefit of prototyping and the need to have the database design 'right first time'. Good project control is even more essential as enthusiasm for the facilities and prototyping can lead to 'over designed' solutions.

- It proved necessary to allow for the learning curve for 'traditional programmers'. Some of the traditional definitions of project phases tend to become blurred, e.g. the aspect of training experienced during the workshops. It is particularly important that all programmers understand how the 4GL applies record locking or multi-user problems may be experienced.

- Finally, it was found that success could bring problems too. As users saw the benefits reaped they tended to expand system boundaries by using arguments that as the IT function could now respond quickly, this 'small' request could be met.

6.4 SUMMARY

Any organization, whether it be in the public or private sector, will resist change to a greater or lesser extent. That is, any organization will have:

- staff who are trained in, and used to, particular working practices;

- investment in existing hardware, whether this be in terms of computer technology or machinery, etc.;

- staff who fear that any change may threaten their job security;

- reasons (whether or not they be sensible ones!) for keeping current practices and systems and not wishing to take even the first steps of any large change.

  The introduction of CASE technology is no different in this respect. The important points to remember when introducing CASE into an organization are as follows.

- Change should be made in an evolutionary, iterative and gradual manner.

- Revolutionary change is a recipe for disaster.

- Get staff commitment: this is vital.

- People are the most important factor in any change scenario.

- Effective staff training is essential.

- Productivity may not arise immediately but long term benefits must be realized.

- New hardware and software must be planned and budgeted for.

- Cost justification is important but may be difficult to put together.

FURTHER READING

Peters, T. (1988) *Thriving on Chaos*, Macmillan, London.

Peters, T. and Waterman R. (1982) *In Search of Excellence*, Harper and Row, London.

Stacey, R. D. (1990) *Dynamic Strategic Management for the 1990s*, Kogan Page, London.

These texts provide detailed approaches to the management of change.

Gilb, T. (1988) *Principles of Software Engineering Management*, Addison Wesley, Wokingham.

This text provides an excellent text on the use of evolutionary techniques in software development.

7

People matter

7.1 THE STAKEHOLDERS

Many innovations in the area of automation and computerization seem paradoxically to lead to a greater emphasis upon the human and manual processes they seek to replace. For example, many of us are familiar with the environmentally friendly paperless computerized office:

Fig. 7.1 The computerized 'paperless' office.

Whilst it might appear that CASE tools provide an increase in automation and therefore should decrease the significance of the human role in the process, the reverse appears to be true. The increase in technical sophistication requires more careful management, the large initial outlay requires enthusiastic senior management backup and belief and the re-training commitment requires the co-operation of the system developers.

To maximize the chances of success, it is necessary to recognize the different stakeholders in the software development process and their aspirations. These are summarized in Table 7.1.

Table 7.1 Stakeholders in the software development process

Stakeholder	Aspirations and fears
Customer	Wants a system with fewest errors that does what they want at the lowest price in the shortest time
	Fears that they may end up paying for expensive tools
Tool user	Wants a tool that makes their job easier, more satisfying and more productive
	Fears that tools may lead to de-skilling and redundancy
Project manager	Wants to deliver on time with fewest errors and to satisfy the customer
	Fears that change may disrupt the time scales and cause problems with the staff
Quality manager	Wants to ensure that the delivered system is error-free and meets the aspirations of the customer
	Fears that the new tool may reduce the individual's attention to detail
Senior management	Wants to see a return on investment
	Wants to see an increase in productivity and quality
	Fears that this may be another IT white elephant

In this chapter we shall consider how each of these desires and fears can be addressed, and then consider some examples where people issues were critical for one reason or another. Later, in Chapter 8, we shall return to some of the themes discussed here and consider the corporate and strategic implications.

7.1.1 Customers

To consider the role of the customer in the success or otherwise of the adoption of CASE tools let us return to the reason for adopting tools and methods in the first place. Boehm's work (1981) on the cost of maintenance as a function of the software lifecycle shown in Fig. 2.4, is often used to justify CASE as a solution to the 'software crisis'.

Estimates of the percentage of the software development budget spent on maintenance vary substantially, but it is generally agreed that this figure is far too high, and that by improving the quality of the software development process the number of errors can be reduced. In particular, by eliminating errors earlier in the lifecycle, the cost of fixing errors can be reduced.

The means of achieving this improvement, it is suggested, is the adoption of CASE tools and methods. Whilst there are clearly benefits to be gained in this area, a little care is needed in assessing their impact.

Consider first the number or errors. What is maintenance? Maintenance effort is required when the system fails to perform in the way that the customer wants. This may arise from one of two cases:

- Non-conformance to specification. The code departs from its specification in performance. This corresponds to your traditional 'bug'.

- Inaccurate specification. The specification does not accurately reflect the needs of the customer.

Structured methods were introduced originally to deal with the first type of problem through the management of complexity. Their modern counterparts, the methods at the heart of CASE tools, still reflect this. There is an increasing awareness that much of the maintenance effort arises from inaccurate specifications rather than coding errors. As CASE tools improve and move towards better automated code generation, this will become even more apparent.

These problems arise because of a lack of communication between the system designers and the system users, illustrated in Fig. 7.2. The extent of this problem was highlighted by one of the authors in a study which showed that in the large companies visited, there was little or no dialogue between systems providers and system users (Gillies, 1992a).

Fig. 7.2 Communication is crucial in establishing customer needs.

Some CASE vendors have suggested that the diagramming tools provided with their products can provide a media for meaningful communication between customers and developers. This idea has been tested by one of the authors with little success. Whilst an entity-relationship diagram, for example, provides a useful representation for a system developer, it is not generally understood by non-technical personnel. The nature of an information model has little meaning for them.

What has been shown to be useful are rapid prototyping tools which provide a quick and easy way to show customers the look and feel of the product. This can further provide a basis for discussion which, if properly handled, can draw from the user much useful information beyond simple look and feel. Unfortunately, some CASE vendors seem to regard such tools as peripheral at best to the main toolset provided.

Long term user satisfaction depends more upon a deeper understanding of the needs of users and their problem. However, the problem is not essentially one of technology; it is one of motivation on the part of the system developer. They need to recognize that the customer has knowledge of the problem and the requirements of the system which can save much time in the longer term. This need to get the specification right at the start has been highlighted by Boehm (1981) in his graph of the cost of fixing an error as a function of the stage of the development life cycle, cited in Part One.

Thus errors fixed or prevented at the analysis phase represent a huge saving for the company. Although, with the arrival of automated code generation and other CASE tools, the fixing of errors later in the life cycle has become easier and cheaper, prevention rather than cure is still the best choice for cost control and customer satisfaction.

Errors arising from incorrect implementation of the specification leading to system crashes or bugs are just as irritating to the customer as errors in the specification itself. CASE tools and methods have the potential to make a significant impact here. In particular, the use of automated code generation offers the possibility of an error-free representation of the specification in code. Again, this is yet to be realized in practice, but continuing improvements in technology make this a realistic possibility.

In this analysis thus far we have considered the customer as a homogeneous group. However, the customers may be classified in two ways, as shown in Fig. 7.3.

	Internal	External
User		
Manager		

Fig. 7.3 Customer matrix.

a) Internal vs. external customers
The principal advantage of the customer being inside the organization is that there would appear to be a greater opportunity to develop a co-operative relationship between system developers and system users. This

should provide better systems for the users and more understanding of the needs of the system developers in providing such.

However, a study of such organizations (Gillies, 1992a) reveals that this is simply not the case. There appears to be a complacency in the attitude of many such departments towards their customers.

This is reinforced by other work (Davis *et al.,* 1993) looking at the adoption of systematic quality assurance procedures which showed that the percentage of companies supplying IT systems and services to external customers adopting certificated quality procedures is considerably higher (58%) than in internal information systems departments (12%).

The suppliers providing systems to external customers have to be seen to be trying to overcome their natural disadvantage in knowledge of the customers' business. However, whether this is a genuine concern and whether there is time in the average contract to gain sufficient understanding remains to be seen.

b) Users vs. managers

The second distinction which must be made amongst customers is between users and managers. Whilst both have interests in common, their priorities tend to be different. The manager customer has more power in the overall process. They want a successful outcome but are constrained by factors of budget and time and often therefore take a shorter term view of what is required.

The user of the end system is more concerned with long term satisfaction and is therefore more willing to accept a longer time scale if it results in improvements to the system. However, they often have little say in the process and this can lead to problems in the longer term as managers accept compromise to get a system in place on time and within budget.

7.1.2 Tool user

The user of the tool may not be very enthusiastic about it. This negative response may arise from one of a number of reasons:

- Fear;

- Resentment;

- A perceived lack of training.

These are illustrated in Fig. 7.4.

Fear....................Resentment.........What, no training at all?

Fig. 7.4 Reasons for a negative response.

Any change is likely to inspire insecurity. The introduction of automated or semi-automated tools to the software development represents for the IT community what the IT community has been doing for years to other people. Therefore, the system developers know the likely outcome.

The general reasoning behind the introduction of tools and methods is that it will increase productivity. Potentially, if this is realized, then this may reduce the need for programmers and result in redundancies. This provides a basic insecurity regarding the introduction of the technology.

Additionally, there is an implicit reflection upon the professional integrity of the personnel if the tools and methods are being introduced to address a perceived problem. Whilst it is not possible to eliminate these fears and insecurities completely, it is essential to gain the co-operation of the people who are going to use the tools and this may be assisted by a conscious attempt to manage their anxieties.

First of all, there must be adequate explanation and training. No amount of accurate information is as intimidating as a lack of information. The training should emphasize three messages.

The first is that the tools are simply there to enable them to make better use of the underlying methods and to automate the tedious parts of their job. The system has a decision support role rather than a decision-making role. They should make life easier and the tool never takes away the need for judgement and expertise.

The potentially greater threat to their current working practices lies in the underlying method. Therefore, the second point to be made is that the CASE methods represent not a revolution in software design but an evolution from the existing structured methods of which they almost certainly are already aware.

The final message should perhaps not be communicated so forcefully. To address the concerns of staff regarding de-skilling and professional integrity, it may be pointed out that developers familiar with state of the art tools and methods are a highly valued resource within the market place and that this change may greatly enhance their professional development. If this point is made too vigorously, it may lead to problems for the project manager, considered below.

7.1.3 Project manager

The project manager has perhaps the most difficult job of all. They have to balance the pressures from all sides without having the overall authority of their more senior management colleagues (Table 7.2).

Table 7.2 The project manager's dilemma

Stakeholder	Expectation of the project and project manager
Managing customer	They want the project on time in budget and working
User customers	They want a system which meets their aspirations and needs
Development staff	They want to be left to do their job
Quality manager	They want the system to conform to their quality procedures
Senior management	They want the introduction of the CASE methods and tools to go smoothly

They carry much of the responsibility but have little ultimate authority. They may well regard the introduction of CASE tools as another pressure imposed upon them.

The role of the project manager is to try to ensure that all interests are represented and that a proper balance is achieved between the different factors. They must balance the short and the long term view. The short term view says that the project must be completed on time and that this must take priority over all other factors. The longer term view says that the tools and methods must be properly integrated into working practice and that the project must be satisfactory in the longer term.

They must balance the need to keep their project team happy and motivated whilst ensuring that the required level of change is introduced. Further, they must endeavour to ensure continuity of staff so that expertise gained is retained.

As Fig. 7.5 illustrates, if they fail there are plenty of people waiting to pounce. Finally, the project manager must be absolutely convinced of the merits and benefits of the methods, tools and management procedures adopted. Otherwise they will find it impossible to convince the others.

Fig. 7.5 The project manager is pulled in many different directions.

7.1.4 Quality manager

Fig. 7.6 40% of companies surveyed had no QA function at all.

Many companies probably do not have a quality manager! In a recent survey (Davis *et al.,* 1993), over 40% of companies did not even claim to have a QA function for software development. However, it is to be hoped that the companies considering CASE tools and methods are among the more enlightened.

Like the project manager, the quality manager must also balance short and long term goals. In the long term, their job concerning the implementation of CASE is to integrate the new working methods and practices into an overall scheme which will provide improved quality to the customer. The introduction of CASE methods and tools should in the long term assist in at least some areas of quality.

However, the short term effects are likely to be quite the reverse. Disruption of existing practice will result in longer time scales reflected in slower delivery to the customer. Unfamiliarity with tools in the short term is likely to increase errors and bugs. New working practices may invalidate existing acquired wisdom on quality issues.

The quality manager should be a useful resource in what is a difficult time for the organization. They should have experience of managing change and introducing new working practices.

In any organization where thought has been given to improving the quality of software, the introduction of CASE tools and methods should be seen as part of the process of continual improvement. In fact, this is true of any organization. In an organization without a quality improvement process, the introduction of a CASE method and tool can only have a limited impact.

7.1.5 Senior management

'The future of this company is IT. I am behind you 100%.'

Fig. 7.7 A lack of genuine senior management support can kill any project.

In any innovation within an organization, the support of senior management is crucial. Everyone seems to have worked in an organization at some time where an edict has come down from on high only to be followed by practical experience that shows that it is a case (CASE?) of 'do as I say not as I do'. Nothing kills an innovation more quickly than this senior management hypocrisy.

However, there are also specific reasons why CASE tools and methods require particular support if they are to succeed. Principal amongst these is the long time scale before benefits are realized. There will be a period during which quality will fall, productivity will fall and there will inevitably be pressure on management to reverse the changes that have been made.

Only if the support for the new working practices goes right to the top will the organization persevere with CASE at this stage. Other managers within the organization simply do not have the authority to carry things through. In particular, the project managers, if committed to the new methods themselves, must feel that in a crisis they will receive the backing of the senior management.

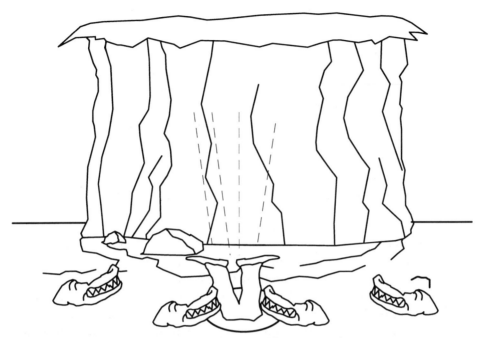

Fig. 7.8 Without senior backing other managers will not succeed.

The level of commitment of senior management may be gauged at the start of the project if the short term problems are adequately presented. It is disastrous to avoid these issues in presentations to senior management in order to push the project through, as this support will evaporate at the first sign of short term problems.

However, for senior managers themselves, there remains the fundamental issue of whether they should support the adoption of CASE and its associated investment. In simple terms, the answer is that CASE is not an end in itself but a means to achieving better systems. It is therefore only worthy of support as part of an overall strategy to enable the IT function to meet business needs better. The content of that strategy is discussed in Chapter 8.

7.2 CASE STUDIES

7.2.1 The pallet company

The first example is a successful company which produces wooden pallets. It has at its disposal the resources of 35 people, 300 customers,

2000 stock lines, 11 items of manufacturing plant and approximately £½M of employed financial resources. It has 1000 different pallet types, produces 700 000 pallets per year giving a sales value of £3.5M and operates a 'just in time' system for deliveries of pallets on demand.

The company, whilst being heavily involved in manufacturing, believes it is a service operation. It is important to recognize that a pallet is not just a pallet but part of the unit load. The unit load consists of the design of the pallet for particular customers, the loads to be carried, the shrink wrap, the securing method and the method of movement of the pallet. It is the company's commercial strategy to become the recognized experts in the provision of efficient design and supply of unit load equipment.

The company believes that IT has an integral part to play in the realization of the commercial strategy. It also believes that it is necessary that all people in the company are convinced of the benefits of IT, not only to the company, but to their own personal development. To this end the company has invested heavily in IT. They installed an off-the-shelf accounting package in 1983. This was followed by the development of a bespoke production control and costing system in 1985 and a customer care system in 1987.

7.2.2 The systems

The production control and costing system was a bespoke system because off-the-shelf packages available at the time would have required much customization and a change in working practices. The system has provided numerous benefits for the company and has amply repaid the investment in its development. Profits have gone up 20% per year over a five year period. The price of the bespoke system was similar to off-the-shelf packages and the total system's cost, hardware and software, was approximately £30 000.

The customer care system contains all the information that relates directly to the customer. If a member of staff is in telephone contact with a customer all the information is immediately accessible to answer any questions concerning the status of their orders. Working in tandem with the customer care system, and integrated with it, is the management information and forecasting system which takes information from the customer care system and prepares a wide variety of analyses. These analyses provide the company with information such as profitability of customers, sales people, products, industry sector, forecast against actual sales, direct labour cost, materials cost and gross profit. The total system cost, hardware and software, was approximately £40 000.

The bespoke systems were developed using a software prototyping method. The problem was discussed between the system developer and the managers and users. Software engineering methods were used to build a model of the business. The model of the business consisted of a data model (entity-relationship) and a process model (data flow diagram). These graphical models were used as the main communication between the company and the consultants. They helped to gain an understanding of how the company worked before the construction of the computer system started. The business model was then entered into a CASE tool called SOURCEWRITER, which generated the computer software. The computer software was then used by the users to ensure it was producing what was required.

After further discussion between the users and the systems developers the business model was altered and the cycle repeated. The verification loop to the system designer ensures that the system is built correctly, whilst the validation loop between the software and users ensures that the right system is built. This development method, using a CASE tool, guarantees that the engineered software system is what the users require, and not what the system developers thought they required.

7.2.3 Reasons for success

There were other reasons for the success of the two bespoke systems. The most important was strong top leadership involvement, with the Chief Executive Officer driving the project forward, not doing it but driving it! Through good communications the committed users in the organization are completely sold on the idea of succeeding with IT. This suggests that small companies who do not have staff with IT knowledge should seek expert advice.

This is not the end of the story. The future plans are to link the systems and provide a completely integrated data base of information throughout the company. They also intend to allow their customers to access the computer systems so that they can see the status of their orders. They believe that they will have to appoint an IT manager who will become as vital as the accountant in the running of the business.

7.2.4 The company

The second company in this section is a US toy manufacturer, owned by a larger more diverse organization. Their toys have been available in the UK since the early 1930s, but there were no significant sales until the early to mid 1970s, when both the UK and Continental markets were developed through distributors. Growth has been rapid, and today's organization, with European sales of around 70m per year, consists of two manufacturing/distribution sites in the UK and Belgium, and sales companies in the main markets of UK, France, Germany, Benelux, Spain and Italy.

In the mid-1980s, the decision was taken to replace all current System 34 systems with System 38. Re-development of the sales and distribution systems followed. Live running began two years later at the first site at Peterlee in County Durham. The remaining sites in Belgium, France and Germany were due to start live running one year later.

7.2.5 The background

The business systems had been running since the beginning of 1983. These were designed as integrated single site systems, i.e. on the basis that each site was operating as a separate unit. Since then operations and management have become far more centralized, particularly in the areas of stock and distribution. Systems have been adapted, but they are, nevertheless, running in a way for which they were not originally designed.

Re-development was, therefore, needed to overcome existing problems and to bring systems into line with current business needs. A secondary aim was to improve the general use and effectiveness of IT in the company.

7.2.6 The scope of the project

The sales and distribution systems cover the following business applications:

- order processing and invoicing

- stock control and distribution

- customer accounting

- sales and order statistics.

A single, integrated system has been developed, which will support all the company's sales sites. It is run on a centrally located System 38, with remote sites linked by leased lines.

7.2.7 The use of software engineering tools

In the short term, most of the difficulties facing the development team arose from the rapid change of technical environment, combined with tight deadlines.

- Live running was scheduled for just 18 months after delivery of the hardware. This left little time to assimilate the new environment, analyse the requirements of a multi-national user community, design and code the new systems.

- System 34 and System 38 were found to be radically different environments. This difference was accentuated by the change from COBOL to RPG III. Coding ability was, therefore, significantly weakened: overnight the accumulated reservoir of COBOL code was lost: RPG coding has to be started from scratch.

- Revisions to design and specifications were constantly required, both because of improving technical knowledge, and (as with any project) changing user requirements.

The traditional long term problems that were faced included aligning systems to the needs of the business, a quicker response to user requests and a growing application backlog.

Having identified a coding bottleneck, it was decided to investigate automatic code generation. With only a short time available, and as only two viable products were known, the selection process was simple and short. From a preliminary examination one product was selected and set up for a two month trial period with full time usage by four development staff. From this, it was decided to continue its use for the whole project.

The following conclusions were drawn:

- As the product was designed as an expert system, the knowledge base could continue to be increased and refined. This would allow inefficient code to be controlled.

- A reduction in program coding time was achievable. This included complex programs.

- Programs, files and fields could all be designed, specified and documented through the product.

The justification, therefore, was that, for a relatively modest cost, the company would at least be able to generate skeleton code to replace the missing COBOL reservoir; at best they could be laying the foundations for a productive 4th generation environment.

7.2.8 The issues and challenges

Overall, there was a very positive staff attitude to the use of the tools: it was apparent early on that development staff would not be 'de-skilled', and that a good level of technical expertise was still required. In addition, a high proportion of staff were involved, thus avoiding the feeling of an 'exclusive' pilot project. Although relatively little training was required to learn basic use of the tool, there was a heavy learning curve for its effective use. Consequently, there were initial losses in productivity, resulting in some problems of morale.

One significant side effect of the tool was the integration of the specification and coding processes. This did help to speed up development, but also proved a problem at first. Time was lost in preparing a traditional detailed specification, and using the tool to try to reproduce the required code. Instead a more functional outline specification was needed, enabling the tool to function more as the detail program designer. The project team had to learn to work with the tools rather than against them, which did require a change in approach by both data-processing and user staff.

All interactive programs were developed using the tools. However, not all applications were totally suited to automated development, and some time could have been saved if more selectivity had been employed. In particular, some applications would have been developed more efficiently through generation of a skeleton, followed by manual completion. Some programs where development was 'forced' have had response time problems in the live environment.

Within the project, estimating and control has been a constant problem. New, simplified project control and reporting procedures had to be developed to cope with the new environment.

The benefits to the company are seen as better planning, a change in working practices resulting in better design, a more functional approach to systems development and standardized code produced more quickly.

7.2.9 One year later

The new systems were implemented on schedule. Twelve months later, the systems were due to be implemented at all the company's European sites. However, this remaining development was almost all batch work, and use of the 4GL tool was consequently at a very low level. Coupled with this, most of the technical staff who had worked on the project had by this stage left the company, leaving nobody with in-depth knowledge of the product. The company were, therefore, facing a total re-build of their environment.

One fact is very apparent. Whatever the environment, 4GL or otherwise, success depends on recruiting and holding the right staff. This company failed to retain the staff and therefore lost the expertise gained. During the year, however, they had gathered enough experience to recognize the potential benefits of software engineering methods and tools. They therefore faced the task of reviving their 4GL environment, following the European implementation programme.

7.3 SUMMARY

In this chapter, we have considered the roles of people within the software development process and seen how they are affected by the introduction of CASE methods and tools.

We have also considered how their own fears and aspirations can control their response, and have suggested ways that these may be managed to increase the probability of a successful outcome. The first case study has illustrated the importance of top management support. The second shows how an apparently successful implementation can be stopped in its tracks if the staff and their associated acquired expertise cannot be retained.

The lesson which must be learnt if tools and methods are to lead to successful solutions is that people matter. Each of the stakeholders in the process has their own aspirations and fears. The management of these aspirations and fears is crucial to the successful implementation of CASE tools and methods. This has several consequences for the adoption of CASE methods and tools:

- Common business and technology objectives must be defined and worked towards by different individuals or organizations including IT and user personnel.

- Leadership and staff motivation are vital if these objectives are to be met.

- Staff must be enabled to work efficiently in producing quality systems. This means including the working environment which research has shown to be so critical, the necessary finance and the technology, otherwise known as methods and tools.

- Training is crucial.

- IT is introduced in the form of projects so that the administrative techniques of project management are part of the engineering process.

- The introduction of new methods and tools involves change, and hand in glove with change goes the associated risk, so that the management of the two is an intrinsic part of the development process.

Software engineering is not just a question of methods and tools. It is the management of people and the effect of change upon them.

FURTHER READING

The texts listed at the end of Chapter 6 by Peters (1988), Peters and Waterman (1982) and Stacey (1990) are also relevant here. In addition, the introduction of quality management ideas is dealt with in Chapter 7 of

Gillies, A.C (1992) *Software quality: theory and management,* Chapman & Hall, London.

8

Consultants can help*

8.1 CONSULTANTS: WHO NEEDS THEM?

In an ideal world there would be no consultants. The need for consultants is a response to a number of problems facing the potential user of CASE tools and methods:

- Expertise in the use of methods and particularly tools is scarce and therefore expensive.

- Expertise is acquired through use, and therefore by definition new users are lacking in expertise.

- Current methods and tools are not intuitive and do not guide the user sufficiently to enable new users to avoid pitfalls.

In short, there is a need for an expert in the use of tools to assist new users until such expertise is acquired by the users. However, whilst an external consultant may understand the method and tool to be used, they will not have a detailed knowledge of the problem domain and the nature of the business. Therefore, they must acquire knowledge as well as impart it.

In this chapter we shall consider the case where a consultant is brought in not simply to implement a system using CASE, but rather to assist in the establishment of CASE methods and tools for use by the organization themselves.

---

* The authors would like to acknowledge the contribution of Paul Ross and Colin Hardy to the material presented in this chapter.

8.2 THE ROLE OF THE CONSULTANT

8.2.1 Bridging the knowledge gap

Fig. 8.1 Consultants can seem expensive.

The first image that the word 'consultant' conjures up in anyone's mind will usually vary depending upon their previous experience (or lack of experience) of the use of such people.

That is, they may view consultants as useful, widely experienced individuals who can bring their vast experience to bear on the problem in hand, and thus produce a quality and cost-effective solution. On the other hand (and at the opposite end of the spectrum) they may view a consultant as a very expensive alternative to doing the job oneself!

There are, however, considerable gains to be made by employing the skills of an effective consultant, provided that they are effective. The key problem facing a consultant is the 'knowledge gap' that exists between themselves and their customer. They must acquire knowledge of the problem domain itself in order to apply their own expertise effectively. This problem of knowledge acquisition has been much studied in the specific context of acquiring knowledge for the development of expert systems (Hart, 1989). However, the subject of knowledge acquisition has now grown beyond this specific area and the techniques are widely applied in a variety of applications.

Fig. 8.2 First capture your knowledge. A good consultant will listen!

8.2.2 Knowledge acquisition

The process of knowledge acquisition is the first stage of knowledge engineering in the same way that requirements analysis is the first stage of software engineering. Thus the consultant requires many of the same skills as a knowledge engineer.

However, unlike a systems analyst or a knowledge engineer building a system, the consultant assisting others to use CASE tools does not have as his primary goal a set of requirements or collection of heuristics. Instead their role is to gather knowledge about the problem domain, combine it with knowledge about the use of the specific method and tool to be used and increase the expertise of the users of the tool to the point where they can become effective users of the tool themselves.

If a consultant simply comes in and carries out the job of using the tool without imparting knowledge, then the next time the tool is required, the consultant will be required again. Thus, the role of the consultant requires technical, interpersonal, organizational and managerial skills.

McGraw and Briggs (1989) have constructed a wish list of knowledge engineer skills, which includes the following attributes:

- fast learner

- effective communicator

- knowledge acquisition techniques

- organized, good record-keeper

- conceptualises well

- knowledge in many diverse areas.

To this we may add a number of additional skills specific to our CASE consultant:

- ability to impart knowledge

- detailed knowledge of the CASE tool and method.

They note that many of the tasks carried out by knowledge engineers are identical or similar to those associated with consultants in more conventional computer based information systems, i.e.

- analysing information flow

- determining program structure

- working with experts to obtain information

- performing design functions.

The role of CASE consultant requires a skill mix which overlaps the traditional role of analyst and programmer combining the interpersonal skills of the analyst with the technical skills of a programmer. In a survey recently of the requirements of knowledge engineering, seen similarly as requiring a broader skill mix than traditional systems analysis or programming, Awad (1992) identified the following skills:

- part systems analyst

- part psychologist

- part interviewer

- part problem solver

- experience

- logical reasoning capabilities

- communication skills

- team working

- working with domain experts

- programming skills

- creativity

- dealing with uncertainty during information gathering.

Awad and Lindgren (1992) also note that many of the personality traits of the successful knowledge engineer are similar to those of any good consultant, and they cite the following as important factors

- creativity

- intelligence

- an ability to think logically

- pragmatism

- responsibility.

The knowledge engineer clearly performs a function that is in many ways very similar to that of the systems analyst: however, in addition to the usual system development tasks of dealing with users and management, a major role for the knowledge engineer is to elicit knowledge from an expert, who is hopefully a willing participant in the system development process (but might not be!).

So the knowledge engineer must have the interpersonal skills and experience to facilitate the management of expert egos, reluctant participants, personality clashes and so on.

Our CASE consultant must do all of this if he wishes to acquire the knowledge of the business he requires, and be able to impart knowledge as well. The cost of a good consultant may start to seem more reasonable in the light of these requirements.

8.2.3 Benefits

We have all heard horror stories about the expensive consultants who cost a lot and gave little in return. However, in practice a good consultant will bring a number of benefits.

They should have a wide range of experiences, from a wide and differing range of companies and market sectors. All of these experiences can be brought to bear in the solution of your problem. They will be impartial, and not involved in internal politics and will not have a particular 'axe to grind'.

Fig. 8.3 Consultants are above internal politics and have no axe to grind.

They will have time to devote solely to the project. If you devote one of your own people to it, it is quite likely that they will also have every day company matters to deal with. A consultant will be a member of a professional body, and will have to adhere to certain professional codes of conduct.

8.2.4 Choosing a consultant

The previous sections have highlighted the wide range of skills required by consultants. Many people tend to feel that the consultants that they employ are overpaid and not up to the job. It is therefore essential to find an appropriate and competent consultant for your needs.

A consultant may be perfectly competent but inappropriate for your needs. For example, a consultant who has only had experience of the London Stock Exchange is unlikely to be appropriate for the needs of a philanthropic housing association.

Similarly, a consultant may be appropriate but incompetent. It is a sad fact that many people who have high ethical ideals and might be very sympathetic to the aims of the organization have no idea how a business needs to operate.

Table 8.1 summarizes the criteria for selecting a consultant for appropriateness and competence.

8.3 CASE STUDIES

The case studies describe a range of experiences with consultants, from a traditional knowledge acquisition project which led to an implemented system to examples where the consultants enabled the organizations to implement CASE methods and tools.

8.3.1 A knowledge-based system (KBS) for fault diagnosis

The client company in this case study is a machine intensive operation, manufacturing plastic containers, using an extrusion thermo-forming process. They represent one company within an international federation of companies associated with the manufacture and distribution of vending and food services packaging.

Each stage of the products manufacture is handled by the company, from the raw materials to packaging and distribution. One of its central concerns, which keeps it in line with BS5750 (a quality management standard discussed in Chapter 12), is the quality of the product.

Table 8.1 Selecting a consultant

Area	Criteria	Considerations
Appropriateness	Experience	Where has the consultant gained experience? Increasingly consultancy companies are recruiting practitioners and training them in CASE methods and tools.
	Skills	Are their skills transferable to your domain? Where the consultant has demonstrated capability in a related area, their skills are more likely to be applicable.
	Culture	Have they worked in similar organizations? Since the consultants will be working closely with your existing staff it is important that they fit in with the existing organizational culture.
Competence	Experience	How much actual experience do they have? Since the consultants are coming in as 'experts', it is reasonable to assume that they should be able to demonstrate adequate experience.
	Skills	Do they have the required mix of skills? As has been stated, the required skill mix is broad. However, since consultants command high fees, they should provide the requisite skill mix.
	References	Can they provide names of satisfied customers? There is no substitute for a personal recommendation. Ideally, this would be someone known to you, but failing that they should be able to name reference sites.
	Professionalism	Consultants should be members of a professional body. This should guarantee minimum standards of behaviour and performance and provide a mechanism for resolving any disputes which may arise in the worst cases.

This is monitored manually both by the operator and the Quality Assurance Department. Since the output of these machines can exceed 80 000 items per hour, it is also financially critical to keep the product within specification, and thus avoid down-time.

The operators at the user company were sufficiently well trained to be able to deal with a limited number of clearly defined product-based problems. However, when problems were unfamiliar, or did not respond to initial adjustments, expert diagnosis was obtained either from more experienced operators or from production or development personnel. As is typical of such situations, having to bring someone in takes valuable time, and takes the expert away from whatever they were involved in.

The task was, therefore, to develop a knowledge based diagnosis system that could be used primarily by the operators to assist in their operations. The user company also hoped to use the software as evidence of the potential of knowledge based system development within the company, and possibly the group.

A consultant was appointed to determine the knowledge required by such a system and implement a system based upon that knowledge. Their main point of contact in the user company was an experienced middle manager; consequently, he was the individual who determined the main character of the KBS to be developed. The consultant also had contact with two other employees, a production engineer and an experienced operator/trainer.

All three were involved in knowledge acquisition sessions, but it was the production engineer who was used as the key expert within the development. The specification of the problem domain was assisted by the fact that the project engineer had been given responsibility for a particular machine within the production line. This machine, which puts the curled lip on vending machine cups, performs its role immediately before packaging. Consequently, this was a vital location to determine those problems which were large enough to damage the product, but may have slipped through the checks carried out by the operator up to that point.

Whilst visually the problems affecting the cups are not large, the product is flawed, and can lead to customer dissatisfaction. It is also probably the hardest point to determine the cause of the problem, since it could feasibly have been caused at any of one or more points throughout the process.

There are nine typical problems that can occur to a cup, that would be picked up at the rim curler. In discussion with the experts, it was decided to break these problems down into three phases, each dealing with three problems. For the KBS, it was decided to deal with one phase, which covered the three most common problems; a hot wrinkle, which is generally caused by the melting of a thin product; an open curl, which to a large extent, is the opposite of hot wrinkle; and dust or hairs, associated with scuffing or poor trimming of the rim.

Using a client-centred approach meant that the consultant needed a clear understanding not only of the problem areas, but also of what the client wanted the system to do. From their descriptions, it was apparent that what they required was a system that standardized the procedures used by the experts and senior operators in their diagnosis of particular problems. This suggested a decision tree model.

A decision tree approach does not necessarily require that the system contain the problem solving heuristics of the expert. It operates on the principle that an expert applies their heuristics to a given problem, and that the resultant decisions are coded. This generates a representation where the decisions are 'hard-wired'; that is, all possible responses from the system are coded. This type of model is relatively easy to develop compared to eliciting and then representing expert heuristics, which are often difficult to articulate.

Software development was undertaken in Crystal. Crystal is an expert system shell which offers a large number of in-built menu-driven functions. Although its inference mechanism is one of backward chaining, its basic operation is one of a decision tree. This fitted well with the knowledge representation mechanism chosen for the KBS.

Crystal allowed the consultant to create a knowledge based system whose size and complexity exceeded the demands of the user company. The central knowledge base consisted of 1407 commands in 402 rules, using 139 variables. There were four product specification knowledge bases with their associated export files, and the file used to hold the form feed variable.

In this case study the software appears to have exceeded the expectations made of it, and the project was very successful. Although the main reason for the success was undoubtedly the skills and abilities of the consultant concerned, the experts whose knowledge was acquired were also extremely keen to assist in the process. The outcome may well have been otherwise, had there been problems in acquiring the knowledge.

Although the purpose of knowledge acquisition in this case was to implement a system, it was dependent upon the process of knowledge acquisition. It illustrates the importance of identifying key individuals in the company and securing their co-operation.

8.3.2 Commodity trading systems development

The consultancy concerned in this scenario was set up in 1979 and is now established as a leading consultancy for high technology research and innovation in the North of England. It provides a range of consultancy and commercial services in software, hardware development and microelectronics. Current and past research projects involve projects under the UK Alvey programme and the European Esprit and RACE programmes.

In total, the consultancy has 1221 staff with a turnover of over £7M p.a. Involvement in research activities has enabled the consultancy to develop a high level of in-house expertise in a number of methodologies and tools which are applied in their commercial, training and manufacturing operations.

The client company in this scenario was established in 1969 in the North of England, in response to requests from farmers for an efficient and economical centralized grain drying, storing and trading facility which would buy or store grain. Tight margins need efficient administration and cash flow controls.

The rural location restricted the availability of skilled book-keepers and the decision to computerize all the administrative systems was taken in the early 1980s. The consultancy assisted in the completion of this and the user company is today one of the largest grain storage businesses in the country.

By the late 1980s, some system inadequacies had become apparent and the decision was made to develop a new system with an expected future life of five to ten years. Whilst the original development used good software engineering practices, it did not use any tools or core software packages such as a Database Management System (DBMS), Structured Query Language (SQL) and Fourth Generation Languages (4GL).

Based on the consultancy's own constant research and development activities, the use of tools was envisaged in three phases, namely design, implementation and project management.

The consultancy's stated requirement was to identify tools which would increase the productivity and quality of software which was suitable for the complexity of the user company's system and would allow them maximum involvement, simple maintenance, self-documentation and flexible and extensible system development.

After considerable external and in-house research, the consultancy settled on the Yourdon methodology for the design tool, with their expertise leading to reducing risk and the learning curve, because of the short project time scale.

The 4GL used for implementation was selected from a short list including ACCELL, ORACLE, INFORMIX 4GL and SCULPTOR. Each of these was considered to be good in its own right and ACCELL most closely approached the requirements of the user company. For project management purposes, HORNET is used as a standard by the consultancy, and was employed during this project.

The project had a target duration of seven months. Technical complexity, user amendments and price constraints all contributed to an overrun of three elapsed weeks.

The project was recognized to be a learning experience for both the user company and the consultancy, particularly in the areas of the Yourdon design methodology and toolkit and the ACCELL fourth generation language. The Yourdon design toolkit proved to be easy to learn and simple to modify. The toolkit produced consistent and modifiable diagrams whilst providing automatic verification and cross-checking. This in turn produced major productivity gains in the speed of verification and confidence in the system design. The generation of a data dictionary was also considered to be a major advantage.

Whilst the general impression was positive, it should be noted that there were no productivity benefits in initial generation of diagrams and the lack of a data transfer link to the 4GL tool was a disadvantage and a potential source of integrity problems.

The ACCELL 4GL tool used was also popular. The basic features of the system proved easy to learn, although the full features of the 4GL required a lengthy familiarization. Particularly well received were the facilities for screen painting and rapid screen prototyping. On the other hand, the manual entry of database design was somewhat laborious and the design was affected by the capabilities of the 4GL system.

The user company received a larger system of greater functionality, developed over a shorter period and at a lower cost than the previous system. This was due to the successful implementation of the new methods and tools. This success was built upon the effectiveness of the consultants applying their technical expertise to the business problems of the client company. The consultants as well as the clients have learnt from the experience. The tools have contributed to this saving and future developments will benefit more as the consultancy build up their experience and knowledge both in the use of these tools and in the system itself.

8.3.3 IT system design in medium-sized manufacturing companies

The consultant in this case study had been an independent computer consultant and developer of bespoke software for six years before his involvement in these projects. Before that he spent three years in general management, a year teaching, and three years in systems analysis and computer programming.

His main areas of business expertise are in financial control, production control, production scheduling, stock control, sales order processing, purchase order processing and management information systems. He has also been involved with stock-broking and service companies.

Over the last eight years, he has gained experience in software for accounts, stock control, sales order processing, purchase order processing, word-processing, spreadsheets, electronic offices and databases. Nearly all the bespoke software has been written to integrate with packaged accounting software and to meet the requirements of company operations where no suitable packaged software has been available.

This background provided the consultant with a very broad range of skills enabling him to operate effectively as a consultant. This case study describes experiences in helping three manufacturing companies. Company A employs 35 people, has 300 customers, 2000 stock lines and manufactures 1000 pallet types. Eleven main items of manufacturing plant are used to produce 700 000 pallets per annum, and generate £3.5M of sales.

An integrated computer system has been successfully implemented for estimating, sales order processing, stock control, production planning, production control, job costing, bonus calculations, management information, and a very comprehensive customer care system.

The management of the company feels that the computer system has been a major factor in achieving the following benefits:

- Profits were increased by 20% per annum over the last five years.

- Turnover was increased by 15% per annum.

- Stock was reduced by £100 000.

- Instant access was provided to a large volume of customer information.

- Management reports were up-to-date and well presented.

- Period-end accounts were prepared on time.

The computer system consists of approximately 250 programs and 250 000 lines of code, of which 2500 were hand coded. The programs run on a Novell network with 10 terminals and 150Mbyte of on-line storage. Besides the bespoke computer programs, the company uses packaged software for the nominal, sales and purchase ledgers, spreadsheets, small databases, and word-processing.

Companies B and C are also manufacturing companies that have implemented computer systems in similar business areas to Company A, but the systems are completely different in all three cases.

A company's method of operating will be influenced by its market, the products it makes, its method of manufacture, the size of the batches of products that it manufactures and the management style of the directors. All of these factors dictate what the ideal computer system for a company will be like.

Consider sales order processing for the three companies. Company A makes 90% of its production to order and 10% to stock. Most of the raw materials are bought on forecasts of requirements. Company B makes all products to order but keeps stocks of some raw materials based on market forecasts and buys the remainder for customers' orders. Company C makes all products to order and buys all board (its main raw material) for customers' orders. In the business area of sales order processing we obviously have two extremes and a wide variety of cases in the middle. Situations range from buying all raw materials for customers' orders and manufacturing only upon receipt of a customer's order, to forecasting market trends and buying all raw materials and manufacturing according to forecasts.

An effective IT solution requires the planning, design, management and direction of the writing and implementation of a bespoke computer system that meets the company's requirements. The aim in all cases is always to increase the effectiveness, efficiency and profitability of the business, and never to promote 'technical wizardry' for its own sake.

In all three cases described, a structured systems analysis and design method was used to develop the systems. Within the method, use was made of two data modelling techniques, entity-relationship diagrams and data flow diagrams. All the systems discussed are data processing systems. The foundation of these systems is an Entity–Relationship (E–R) model. This is used to define the relationships between the records in the files in the system.

At the same time, businesses are dynamic organizations and are totally dependent on information and data flows. Data flow diagrams are used to show the flow of data through the system.

In most data processing systems, the processing of data at any one point is usually very simple, the complexity is contained in the relationships between the records in the files. By combining the E–R model and the data flow diagram it is possible to build up a very comprehensive picture of the business. At this stage it is often possible to see ways of eliminating superfluous processes from the administration of a business.

In the above companies, a CASE tool was used called SOURCEWRITER. This is a COBOL code generator for developing interactive and report programs. It is primarily a tool for the systems analyst, designer and programmer.

The COBOL/2 Workbench was used for development. This is more than a COBOL compiler: it is a complete COBOL development system. COBOL was selected for the development language because it formed a total product with SOURCEWRITER. It is flexible, standard, has a large range of target machines, and the best compilers are very highly tuned for performance.

The hardware development platform employed was a powerful IBM PC or compatible with a large fixed disk unit. The hardware can run under MS-DOS, OS/2, Novel Netware, or XENIX/UNIX. A total development system of this type which can be used by two or three system developers can be bought for under £10 000. However, before effective use could be made of these tools and techniques, it proved necessary to ensure that a good working relationship existed between managers, computer users, and the computer developers.

Other considerations when selecting development software which had to be taken into consideration included :

• trade-offs between performance and development costs

• run time licence costs

• longevity of suppliers

• longevity of computer code

• ongoing CASE tool development.

Experience has shown that it is unproductive to tune precisely the vast majority of bespoke programs. It is far better to invest in more powerful hardware and improve the performance of all programs in the system. When comparing development systems, run time licences can vary in price. For an eight user system running under Novel Netware, a run time system for COBOL may cost approximately £200, whereas for a typical 4GL it could cost £5000.

The systems developed have all been business system driven, and very specific to the company involved. Users of the system have been totally involved in its development. The CASE tool involved generated bug-free programs. The right business system for the company has been developed and implemented.

SOURCEWRITER proved to be an effective tool. However, there remain a number of limitations found in use. The tool has no facilities for generating batch processing applications. There is no automatic generation of inter-file calculations and there remains a need for hand written code.

There proved to be a learning curve to climb for both users and developers. For the developer, it takes time to master the methods, techniques and CASE tool employed. The user must learn about the development method, and about the management of projects using these tools and techniques.

There are a number of advantages to the consultant or software house. The interactive development process with the client brings benefits in terms of better communication and understanding, leading to greater client loyalty to the project and the product, as well as a product which serves the clients needs better. On the technical side, there are advantages with increased code productivity, less maintenance and easier implementation.

The client, too, has much to gain. The production of a bespoke business system should ensure that the system matches business needs. The client shares the benefits of continuous involvement in development which should result in easier implementation and installation. The result should be a reliable system proving cost-effective through economic development and low maintenance. It should also provide a growth path for the future.

8.3.4 Computer integrated manufacture (CIM) of prestige cars

The consultancy in this case study provides assistance on the effective use of IT, particularly in manufacturing companies. To date their clients include major automotive and aerospace companies, as well as other major private and public concerns. They have also been involved in a number of ESPRIT and Eureka projects in the area of CIM strategy.

There is no universal definition of computer integrated manufacturing (CIM). In simple terms, CIM may be viewed as the effective use of IT in the engineering/manufacturing sector of industry. However, it is possible to lay down three principles   CIM: integration of information, integration of activities and a consistent and coherent approach to the management of the enterprise.

To provide an efficient and responsive enterprise which meets its customer's needs and market demands, the integration of all company activities and information is essential. Information is the company's most valuable asset; it needs to be coherent, accurate and available at all times.

CIM involves the linking/integration of all the business functions in the manufacturing organization to form an efficient, responsive and unified enterprise. Thus, CIM is not a system that you can buy and implement overnight. Companies need to adopt a structured view of their operations if they are to define clear operating procedures and requirements. Furthermore, knowledge about company activities is essential for good management.

There are many benefits which can be derived from a successful implementation of CIM. In the case of the Automotive Company involved in this case study, the following business objectives were identified:

- increase production

- increase inventory turnover

- improve productivity

- reduce lead-time.

These objectives were to be achieved within a five year time scale.

Having established that CIM was a vehicle for achieving these objectives and that a strategy for CIM was required, the need for a methodology to develop and implement CIM was identified.

In this case, IDEF-O modelling was identified as a suitable approach. It is a top-down hierarchical decomposition technique. The results are expressed as better activities, information and material flows, constraints and control management with fewer resources used.

The stages for establishing a CIM strategy (or IT strategy in manufacturing) using IDEF-O modelling may defined like this:

First, it is necessary to establish the business objectives.

Once this has been achieved, then a functional model of the existing company operations should be built, i.e. an 'as is' model. This is a top-down functional model of the company expressed in better information and material flows, better constraint and control mechanisms and fewer resources used.

This model is then subjected to a structured/clinical analysis against the objectives in order to eliminate duplication and other waste and to identify and solve inconsistency. From the above stage, a 'should be' model of the company is constructed, showing how the company should operate to achieve its stated objectives.

This final 'should be' model can be used in various ways. It can assist with the creation of specifications for functional and integration requirements for an IT solution. Additionally, it can be used in the formulation of operating procedures, planning and training requirements and during implementation.

For the purpose of this case study, the automotive company may be split into two sections:

- Corporate, which embodies the strategic/tactical functions of the business; and

- Operations, consisting of a series of mini-factories which make the different sub-assemblies making up the car.

This structure was reflected in the project team in that two groups were formed to undertake the various modelling tasks. A planning group was set up to look at production planning, commercial design and production engineering.

The other group concerned itself with operations, looking at four mini-factories which are representative of the rest. These were engine assembly and test, miscellaneous machining, car body shell and bolt-on items (doors, wipers, etc.).

The final generic 'should be' model was proved and tested in two 'mini-factories', namely the engine assembly and test and miscellaneous machining. The consultancy was contracted again to deliver two prototype software packages, a part program management system and a tool management system.

Miscellaneous machining manufactures a wide range of components. In particular, Cell 11 of the 'mini-factory' produces housings for water pumps. To machine these parts, the computer numerically controlled (CNC) machine tools require, for each part, proven and post-processed part-programs which contain the machining instructions.

These part-programs start life on the CAD/CAM systems when, having designed a part, a tool path is generated and subsequently post-processed ('cross-compiled') for a particular CNC machine tool. This program would then have to be proved using various techniques such as simulation. The requirement was that for each component three copies of a part-program had to be held in a database: two previous versions and a current version. Every time the design of an existing part is modified, the part-program must be modified and proved accordingly.

Given that there are a large number of parts which are subject to design modifications and given the archiving and traceability requirements, there is a need to hold these growing numbers of part-programs and manage their use effectively. Allied with part-program information, tooling information for geometry, type, tool number and life is always required. This tooling information needs to be held and managed in a similar way to the part-programs.

The software development methodology used was based upon the principles of structured analysis and design and was based upon the use of diagramming techniques such as Jackson. The IDEF-O model of the miscellaneous machining provided the framework to produce data flow diagrams and other models necessary for the specification of the software. Because the two packages were prototypes, the emphasis was on improving the quality and productivity of the analysis, design, and specification stages of the software development process.

Prokit WORKBENCH, a proprietary analyst workbench CASE tool supplied by McDonnell Douglas, was chosen to provide the environment for generating data flow diagrams (DFDs), Jackson's diagrams of the various processes and all the software documentation.

As far as the actual strategy and software projects were concerned, it is important to note that they were all completed within time scale and budget and met their functionality. This is in itself a major benefit. Clearly CIM can provide many benefits if a top-down strategic approach is adopted as in this case.

The main ingredients for success in this case were clarity of objective, adoption of a top-down methodology for formulation of an IT strategy and the use of CASE tools for software development.

In this case, the requirements of the clients were very complex involving the automation of manufacturing as well as the computerization of business processes. Without the specific expertise of the consultancy, it seems unlikely that the company could have achieved the required degree of expertise to implement the changes.

The choice of consultants was crucial. By making use of a consultancy with specific expertise and experience in computer-integrated manufacturing the client ensured that the consultancy provided was both appropriate and competent.

8.4 SUMMARY

This chapter has discussed the role which consultants can play in IT system development, and has focused upon four case studies where the use of a consultant has clearly benefited the companies concerned. These benefits have accrued largely as a direct result of the consultant's own high level of expertise in IT system design, and experience of the solution of problems which are of direct relevance to the problem domain in question.

The key points identified are:

- CASE expertise is scarce.

- Consultancy requires a broad mix of skills.

- Choose an appropriate consultant.

- Choose a competent consultant.

- Consultants are not cheap but a good one can prove cost-effective.

- Make sure that you both understand the project to be undertaken.

- Communication between the consultant and the staff of the company is a key issue.

- Set out clear initial objectives.

- The role of the consultant is to impart knowledge as well as to complete the project.

FURTHER READING

Hart, A.E. (1989) *Knowledge acquisition for expert systems* 2nd edn, Chapman & Hall, London,

In spite of its title, this text will be of use to all those acquiring knowledge for whatever purpose.

White, M. and Goldsmith, J. (1990) *Knowledge Engineering: Handbook of Theory and Practice*, Systemsware Corp.

This is the manual of the International Association of Knowledge Engineers (IAKE).

9

The long term view

9.1 THE NEED FOR THE LONG TERM VIEW

The long term view is not always popular in any business. The need to show a profit within a fixed accounting period provides a strong incentive for short term-ism.

The IT community has grown used to a rapid rate of change in technology. This actively discourages a long term view. Many of the business functions already computerized such as accounts, payroll and document production show relatively quick returns on investment through rapid increases in productivity. Thus business customers have come to expect a quick return on their investment.

The computerization of software development is not like these other functions. It is a complex process requiring changes in working practices which will lead initially to a decrease in productivity and quality. Therefore the road to a return on the investment is a long one.

The initial investment is made up of a number of components:

- The cost of tools and associated hardware.

- The cost of consultancy support for the introduction of the above.

- The cost of staff re-training.

- The cost of lower productivity.

- The cost of lower quality.

- The cost of maintenance and upgrades for the tools themselves.

Although this might appear to be a one-off capital investment, only the initial cost of tools is a true one-off capital cost. The remaining costs will be spread over a period, probably a number of years.

Due to the rapid rate of change in the IT environment, evaluation of costs and benefits is rarely carried out. Where people have tried to do so, the comparison is made very difficult by the constantly changing development environment. One Australian study (Low and Jeffrey, 1991) considered the effect of introducing back end CASE tools into an organization. This is potentially less disruptive than adopting fully blown integrated CASE tools.

The study compared the impact of two different tools, in three organizations, and compared the use of the tools with the use of conventional techniques. However, because the second part of the study involved only three projects in two different organizations, we shall discount this and consider only the first part taking 8 CASE-based projects out of a total of 59 within the same organization and using the same tool.

These results show the impact of the use of a back end CASE tool on productivity measured as the mean system size divided by the mean effort over a five year period in the same organization and using the same tool.

In the study, productivity was defined in total hours of staff time including both developer and user staff time, and the system size in terms of function points as defined by Sprouls (1990).

Table 9.1 The impact of a back end CASE tool (after Low and Jeffrey, 1991)

Approach	Systems	Mean effort (man months)	Mean system size (function points)	Mean productivity (function points per staff day)
Manual	51	14.9	164	3.86 ($\sigma = 3.7$)
CASE tool	8	15.0	286	4.15 ($\sigma = 3.7$)

Since this study considered a five year period, one might reasonably consider that the benefits of CASE would be clearly visible, but in spite of a gain in the mean productivity, the large dispersion of the results leads to the conclusion that the results are not statistically significant:

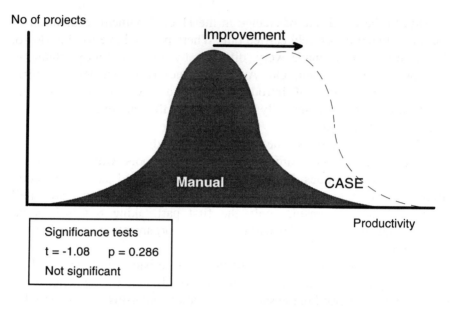

Fig. 9.1 No statistically significant improvements in one study.

Whilst these results are from only one organization, they represent one of the few well-constructed long term studies. The study went on to consider whether the expectation that initial productivity would be lowered was born out in practice. The effort for each project was predicted by a regression line with equation:

$$\text{effort} = 3.143 * (\text{Function points})^{3.835} \tag{9.1}$$

This was compared with the actual effort for each project taken in order of project start. The results, shown in Fig. 9.2, are derived from only 8 projects and cannot therefore be regarded as statistically significant, although they do suggest that productivity increases as experience of CASE tools grows. However, examination of the staff involved in each project reveals that, as in many organizations, the staffing situation is flexible, and that experience of the actual tool users was variable.

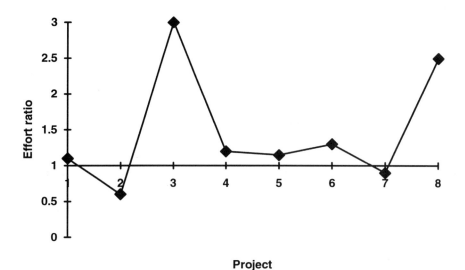

Fig. 9.2 The ratio of predicted versus actual effort for projects in chronological order.

The fit of the regression analysis improves substantially if staff experience is taken into account using a model suggested by Boehm (1981), using a five point scale ranging from 1 (very experienced) through 3 (average) to 5 (very inexperienced). The results are shown in Table 9.2.

Table 9.2 The impact of a back end CASE tool (after Low and Jeffrey,1991)

Factors	Equation	Statistical measures		
		p	*F*	*r2*
size	$e=3.857*(fp)^{3.471}$	3.17	5.39	3.25
size and experience	$e=3.857*(fp)^{3.471}*(xpf)^{3.747}$	3.0022	26.3	3.91

where fp = size in function points
and xpf = experience measured as per Boehm (1981).

Again, the sample of only 8 suggests caution, but the results do suggest that staff experience entering a project plays a major part in the productivity of a project. Projects 3 and 8, the most highly productive by a considerable margin, had by far the most experienced staff:

Table 9.3 Staff experience factor project by project

Project	*1*	*2*	*3*	*4*	*5*	*6*	*7*	*8*
Experience	5	5	1	3	4	3	4	1

where 5 is no relevant experience
and 1 is staff experienced in using tool on recent project.

Low and Jeffrey draw the following conclusions from their own study:

- The introduction of CASE may lead initially to a reduction in productivity.

- Whilst improvements are possible even if staff have little actual experience in the use of the tool, these will be greatly enhanced by effective training prior to the project.

- Higher productivity is achieved when the staff involved have prior experience of the CASE tool.

This empirical study reinforces the view that the initial effects of CASE implementation will be negative. Further, this study deals only with the introduction of back-end CASE tools. The introduction of a fully blown integrated approach involves greater complexity and more people and extends the consequences outside the immediate group of tool users.

One clear advantage of introducing back end tools is that the impact is largely contained within the project teams. Once CASE is introduced into the analysis and design phases of the life cycle the impact affects users as well, the complexity increases and the time to profit increases (Fig. 9.3).

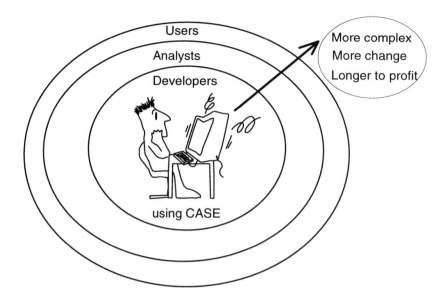

Fig. 9.3 The more change is introduced, the longer to profit.

If the expectation of management is that CASE tools can be introduced on the same time scale as other computerization processes, then the expectations will be disappointed. Whereas computerization in office automation or business transaction can bring immediate benefits and repay investment in a matter of months or at least a year or so, the time-scale for benefits from CASE is measured in years. This is illustrated schematically in Fig. 9.4. The precise time taken will vary according to existing experience of structure methods in general and tools in particular.

The first milestone to be reached, represented by t_1 in Fig. 9.4, is the point at which the tools start to reduce the cost of producing software by lower maintenance and greater productivity.

However, it is only at t_2 that the cost of the initial investment is recouped by the savings made and, therefore, the overall project starts to show a profit. It will be even later before the process can claim a return on the sum invested.

This cost/benefit equation reinforces the need to take a long term view of the process. It also illustrates the importance of senior management commitment, as without this support the project is likely to be aborted before a net benefit can be achieved.

Savings or costs from implementing CASE

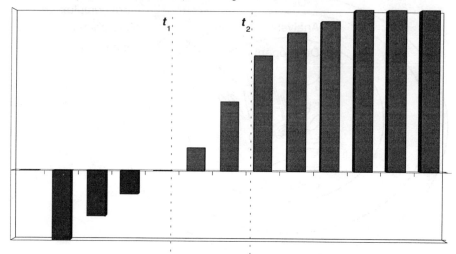

Culmulative savings or costs from implementing CASE

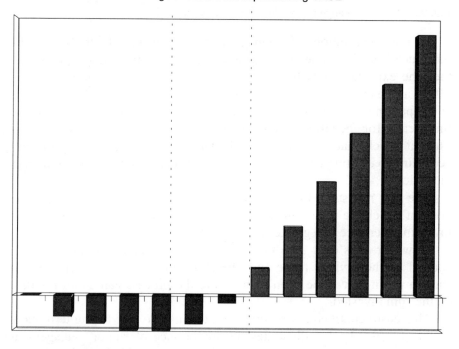

Fig. 9.4 Schematic illustration of the long term payoff of CASE tools.

However, it also suggests that an alternative implementation strategy should be adopted which can bring in benefits more quickly. It has already been suggested that an evolutionary approach to CASE implementation is advisable.

The cost/benefit profile of this kind of approach will be considered next.

9.2 REDUCING THE TIME TO BENEFITS

There are no true short cuts to achieving full benefit from CASE methods and tools. However, by introducing the process in incremental fashion, the costs can be balanced against benefits achieved through partial implementation. Further, the risk of failure is significantly reduced.

The key observation here is that the major benefits from CASE arise not from tools but from the underlying methods. It is also perceived by some users that only if the methods and tool are introduced separately can the underlying methods be properly understood and appreciated. This implies that the greatest long term benefit will be gained from separate introduction of tools and methods. An implementation process of this type is shown in Fig. 9.5.

This type of process may be considered in terms of costs and benefits in three stages. The three principal stages are:

- introduction of methods

- limited automation

- full automation.

The process may be stopped at the end of each of these stages with the benefits accrued up to that stage intact. Some companies may well choose to stop after limited automation, as the third stage offers the most risk and the highest cost.

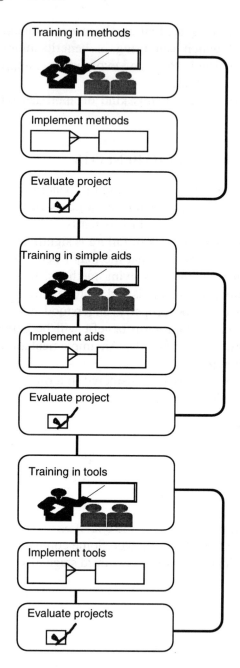

Fig. 9.5 An incremental model of implementation.

Each stage consists of training, implementation and evaluation. The importance of training in gaining productivity benefits is demonstrated by a number of studies including the Australian study. It has also been highlighted that its absence is a major factor in failure.

Its effect upon the cost/saving curve over time is to raise initial cost but reduce time to profit:

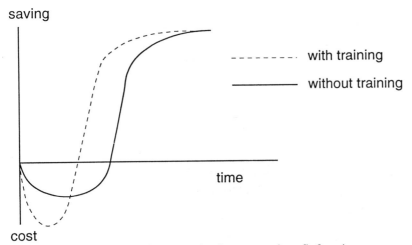

Fig. 9.6 The effect of training upon the time to cost benefit function.

The main costs associated with this phase are training costs and the cost associated with the process of change. However, the amount of knowledge to be assimilated is smaller than a fully blown tool implementation and the degree of change for the developer is less as they do not have to familiarize themselves with the mechanics of a new tool.

Thus this part of the process has a shorter learning time than the fully blown implementation and will quickly start to bring benefits in the form of lower error rates and greater productivity. In particular, although analysis and design may take longer even after familiarization, coding becomes quicker in a short space of time and correction of code in later stages will be streamlined through fewer errors. In an earlier chapter, we have seen how Boehm predicts that the cost of error correction rises logarithmically through the life cycle so that improvements in analysis, even if not seen in productivity rise in this phase, will be reflected in improvements later in development. One company committed to introducing better methods, Sherwood Computer Services, (Gillies, 1992b) introduced SSADM as their CASE method and then, having evaluated suitable tools, did not implement tools but retained paper-based procedures. At a limited cost, they were able to show substantial productivity and quality benefits in a considerably shorter time scale than if they had implemented tools as well. As a consequence, they were able to deliver a new product to the market place on time and within budget.

A further advantage is the ability to evaluate the procedure used and feed back information leading to improvements more quickly than by a fully blown integrated technique.

However, there are still gains to be made by automation. Automation does not however have to be complete. It may also be carried out in incremental stages. The simplest and most cost effective task to automate is the task of diagram production. This may be done using a very simple drawing tool.

Fig. 9.7 Using a drawing tool is effective, but lacks street credibility!

The advantages of this simple automation process are the same as the advantages of basic word processing for document production:

- ease of update and change

- ease of storage

- automatic dating of diagrams

- use of templates and libraries

- little training required.

Because of its simplicity, this automation can bring benefit quickly and therefore cheaply. It has little or no negative disruptive effect upon patterns of working. However, it does have the problem of a lack of credibility.

Other tools of this type are those which fit with manual methods and automate or assist part of the process. One of the attractions of back end CASE tools such as Telon is that they allow programmers to adjust the code and, in particular, to correct small errors which may arise without the need to regenerate the whole piece of code.

A further group of companies has adopted solutions of this kind and made the decision not to proceed further. However, should a full integrated CASE tool implementation be sought, the approach offers a number of advantages over proceeding with a full implementation straight away:

- By the time that a large investment in tools and hardware is required, the benefits should be well established.

- The savings from methods and simple tools can be used to fund further investment.

- The knowledge gained earlier will be invaluable in implementing the full method and tools.

- The knowledge about the method and the tool will be clearly separated, aiding understanding, reducing training times and increasing productivity earlier leading to greater benefits sooner.

The cost benefit function over time is illustrated in Fig. 9.8.

Savings and cost from incremental CASE implementation

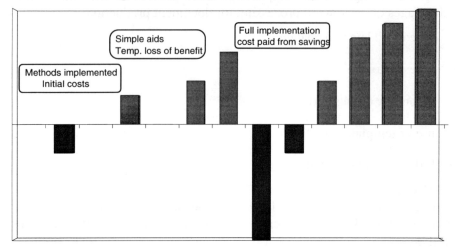

Total savings and costs from incremental CASE implementation

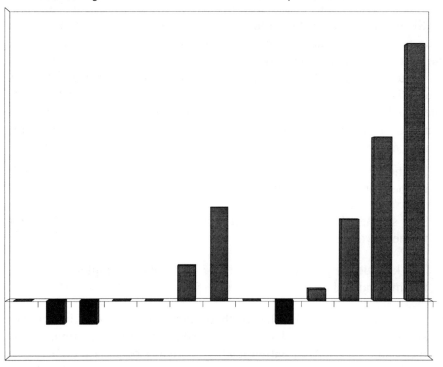

Fig. 9.8 The saving/cost profile for an incremental implementation.

Whatever approach to implementation is adopted, a long term view is required. A clear strategy is required with realistic business goals and associated IT goals.

The 'big bang' implementation of a fully integrated CASE approach is no short cut to the benefits that can be realized and often appears superficially attractive because this is not appreciated.

The following case study describes a CASE success story. It describes the changes within a manufacturing company over a period of seven years. During that time senior management was always committed to the changes and clearly focused upon the long term goals.

9.3 CASE STUDY

The company is a division of the world's leading manufacturer of adhesive backed materials, operating on a 24 hour, 7 day a week basis. To retain its market position and to compete internationally the company needs to improve its customer service constantly through product innovation and quality, delivery reliability and short lead times as well as achieving high levels of plant utilization.

Adhesive backed materials are produced in a two stage manufacturing process. The first stage, termed coating, involves applying an adhesive to the base material and completing the sandwich with a disposable backing material. This backing substrate protects the adhesive until the product is finally used in many diverse applications from the re-badging of the British Airways aircraft fleet to first aid bandages.

After coating, the product is usually in the form of 1000–3500 metre rolls either 1 or 2 metres wide. The second stage of production is called finishing. Here the rolls are either slit and rewound into smaller rolls called cheeses or cut into sheets of various dimensions and packed into boxes. Both sheets and cheeses are subsequently die-cut into labels and finally printed, usually by the customer.

Companies can be found which are good at manufacturing. However, fewer are good at marketing. It is only rarely that companies are good at both.

The company believes that business success stems from a harmonious blend of expert and aggressive marketing combined with innovative exploitation of manufacturing technology. The life blood of this harmony is information, and continuing the analogy, the arteries and veins for its circulation are high quality information systems. Quality systems in this context are systems which answer the needs of the business, both efficiently and effectively.

It is the company's belief, therefore, that marketing, manufacturing and information technology strategies can no longer be developed in isolation. They should be developed proactively and in an integrated fashion to satisfy customer needs, both existing and latent, to gain significant competitive advantage. This has not always been the case.

The company categorizes organizations according to the competitive role of manufacturing and associated information systems (if any). They may be categorized into four grades, summarized in Table 9.4.

Table 9.4 Categories of role of manufacturing

Grade	Description	Characteristics
1	A service to marketing	This type of company is dominated by its marketing department, with the manufacturing function being kept in the dark.
2	Copy industry practice	Manufacturing has rather more status in these companies, but limits its investment to copying the processes and systems of similar companies within its industry sector.
3	Adopt an integrated strategy	At this level, manufacturing has reached the status of having its own recognized strategy which is developed to satisfy the requirements of the marketing, financial and corporate strategies of the company. Although raised in prominence, it still fulfils a reactive as opposed to proactive role in business strategy.
4	Exploit competitive advantage	Companies in this group develop integrated product and market manufacturing strategies. In such cases, manufacturing technology and information systems play a proactive role in repositioning their competitive product within the market.

In 1990, the company was managing the transition from Grade 3 to Grade 4. By contrast, before 1983, they were a very successful Grade 2 company which operated in the high volume commodities and specialities sectors of the industry.

Success came from product and market differentiation strategies which were built upon core skills in marketing and new product development. As European market leaders in their sector, the company's reputation had been built upon providing high quality, innovative products with excellent customer service for which a high premium could be charged.

The business environment changed dramatically in 1983 due to the entry of new competitors from Scandinavia. They had a significantly higher degree of vertical integration from the forest to adhesive labels, together with significant investment in process automation and manufacturing information systems. They were able to move the basis of competition in the commodities sector away from product and market differentiation towards superiority through low cost production. The presence and activities of small focused producers local to their major customers increased the company's need for speed and flexibility of service standards, particularly in distribution. The competitors' activities presented a significant threat to the premiums that could be commanded on service.

To protect its market leadership, the company was forced to reassess its marketing and manufacturing activities and philosophies, together with the role of IT. Up to this point IT had merely provided electronic accountancy systems.

Quality and service objectives were to be met by a multi-million pound investment in process equipment and information systems to achieve computer integrated manufacture by the mid 90s. This was coupled with a policy of non-strategic divestment to optimize the market share/profitability balance. No longer was manufacturing perceived as just a support function to marketing, it was now treated as a strategic weapon of equal or greater firepower.

Manufacturing efficiencies would be gained by the introduction of plant specialization aligned to the needs of specific market segments. Increased service levels would be gained by the implementation of new market-led manufacturing strategies. These would reduce delivery from 6 weeks to a guaranteed 3 – 7 days, whilst maintaining quality and reducing costs.

The successful implementation of these strategies was dependent upon the fast and effective development of new manufacturing information systems for decision support and production control. Unfortunately the company had a centralized data processing department, based in Holland, which was tied to COBOL development within the traditional life cycle.

This meant that:

- Users were generally presented with requirements analysis documents that would have taken months to read yet alone understand.

- Systems development took too long and could not react to the rapid changes in the business environment. Indeed the department was already three years and $4.5m into the development of a particular production control system, which the new strategies would make obsolete.

- There was a great deal of animosity between them and the production plants, in particular the principal UK site.

To achieve this philosophy and implement the desired manufacturing information systems at the principal UK site meant the adoption of in-plant development centres. Essentially, these were manufacturing information centres supported by software engineering methods and productivity tools. They were staffed by business analysts, not technicians. The company chose the bespoke route since prior experience had shown that package solutions needed too much tailoring to the environment and were certainly not the panaceas that the vendors claimed.

In the mid-1980s, the principal UK site installed an IBM Series 1 in what was to become its manufacturing information centre. The PICK operating system was adopted to ensure the potential for maximum user ownership and participation in system design and development. This incorporates a relational database, active data dictionary, screen and line editors, ACCESS, an *ad hoc* query language and an enhanced Databasic programming language. To facilitate fast systems development by business analysts as opposed to programmers, an extremely powerful and easy to use application generator called System Builder was also adopted.

Fig. 9.9 Users were often unable to discuss their requirements.

The method of software development adopted was prototyping of two types, incremental and throw away. These methods were used because users were unable to express their requirements fully in the rapidly changing environment discussed (Fig. 9.9). Indeed, interaction with the system could considerably change requirements.

The company decided to avoid the 'big bang' approach to CIM implementation in favour of pilot studies to assess the viability of the strategies. Without the tools previously discussed, such a development strategy would not have been possible.

At the time of installing the IBM system, the company was experiencing very high levels of scrap in both the coating and finishing operations. Pre-production losses were running at around 6% (of raw material purchases) and coating and finishing scrap at 7–7.5%. Since 1% scrap was equivalent to £250 000 per annum and there were no computerized information systems to address the problem, it was given top priority. It was decided to address the problem using the software engineering method and tools described.

Two business analysis students were given the task of producing a time and materials recording system prototype with on-line shop floor data capture on one of the company's coating lines. Within two months the students had implemented a fully functional prototype system and had trained the production operatives, who had been consulted at every stage of development. This has been used as the basis for the development of a plant-wide time and materials recording system with bar code data collection. This provides the input to a real-time accounting system.

The tremendous success of this project has spurred the development of many other strategic manufacturing information systems, notably:

- CUSA: Customer stock allocation system to support the pilot study of a new manufacturing strategy at the principal UK site.

- FINNET: A networked system for loading and scheduling production on the slitting machines.

With these projects, the company's experience of software development using software engineering methods and tools has grown. This maturity has led the company to adopt front end analysis tools for data modelling to impose more discipline in the development process.

The major benefits that were gained were:

- The methods and tools provided the vehicle to develop production monitoring and control systems very quickly and cost effectively.

- The systems are directly suited to the company's needs whereas package based solutions would have required significant modifications.

- The CAPM learning curve was made easier by being involved in the systems development as opposed to being given a package which would then have required many months of training and modification.

- The company could not have successfully controlled its manufacturing processes in a time of rapid change without fast and flexible information systems development.

- All manufacturing personnel were actively involved throughout the systems life cycle. A recent survey showed a significantly higher degree of user satisfaction with these systems as opposed to those developed using more traditional methods.

- Since the company was entering unknown operating procedures, the system requirements were very ill structured. The methods used coped well with this need for evolutionary systems development.

- The stranglehold of a tradition bound data processing department was broken allowing measures of performance based upon business effectiveness rather than technical effectiveness.

The manufacturing information systems developed over the period described (1983–1990) are now the lifeblood of the company's operations. They have significantly helped the company in maintaining their market leadership. Without them, the company could never have achieved its aim of manufacturing excellence. Equally, without software engineering methods and tools, the systems could not have been developed.

Despite technology and the automation that it can bring, the implementation of CASE, the manner in which it is used and the development of successful systems are entirely dependent upon the people involved, both IT staff and users. If entrenched attitudes had not been changed, then nothing could have been achieved. Hence people, their attitudes and the company culture were the most important considerations in this company's path towards excellence.

What is striking in this case is the company's long term view of success and commitment to long term strategic goals. The projects and benefits described were realized over a seven year period from 1983 to 1990. This long term view enabled them to gain the full advantage of the use of CASE for their information systems and enabled the IT function to support the manufacturing function in pursuit of their goals.

This long term view is an important part of the cultural values needed for a successful CASE implementation, and gaining and keeping people's commitment to long term goals is crucial to success.

9.4 SUMMARY

The crucial message of this chapter is that unlike previous information technologies, the pay-off from CASE will only come in the long term. The benefits will not be seen in the first year or possibly two and the initial costs are high. The time before overall savings are made depends upon the mode of implementation. Although the big bang appears attractive, it is a high risk strategy which may not produce the highest or quickest return.

Crucial to the success in the long term is strong senior management commitment. Without this, the implementation is likely to be aborted before any benefit is seen, possibly at great cost to the company. The lessons from this chapter are:

- CASE tools are expensive and will not provide a quick return on investment.

- A long term strategy is required.

- Senior management must be committed to it.

- Incremental introduction of methods and tools can provide a more cost effective solution.

- Experienced staff produce much greater benefits and must be retained.

FURTHER READING

Low, G.C. and Jeffrey, D.R. (1991) Software development productivity and back end CASE tools, *Information and Software Technology*, **33** (9) 616–621.

The paper provides full details of this Australian study.

Boehm, B. (1981) *Software Engineering Economics*, Prentice-Hall, New York.

This classic text provides a theoretical background for any cost/benefit analysis carried out on software projects.

10

The problem with existing systems

10.1 EXISTING SYSTEMS

When the use of CASE is described, in text books and particularly in the promotional literature associated with a CASE tool it is often assumed that you are designing and implementing a new application with no previous system to replace or current system to be integrated. This is particularly true of the integrated methods and tools designed to cover the whole life cycle, as part of their attractiveness is their self-containedness. By contrast, the SSADM method, designed to cover the analysis and design phases, requires its users to consider first the existing systems.

Very occasionally, such a 'green field site' arises, and the first case study describes such a situation. However far more common is the situation where existing systems are already in place. In the first part of this chapter we shall consider the problem of how to take account of such systems within current CASE technology. In the second, we shall consider reverse engineering which offers the advantages of CASE tools and methods for old and existing systems.

In most cases, a system being implemented replaces an existing information system. The existing system may be not be in the form of a computerized system, but this is of secondary importance. In some cases, the system to be written will have to integrate with other computer systems. In all cases, the system will have to integrate with an existing human system.

CASE methods may be classified according to their starting point, as described in Table 10.1.

Table 10.1 Classification of CASE methods according to starting point

	Front end methods starting with existing systems	*Integrated methods starting with strategic view*
Examples	SSADM	Information Engineering, ORACLE
Advantages	Forces consideration of existing systems	Integrity of approach
	Allows user to implement design with an existing integrated information system	Strategic view
		Elegant solution
Disadvantages	Can lead to piecemeal approach to system design	Code generated is not transparent
	Can inhibit innovative solutions	Difficult or impossible to use in conjunction with existing systems
	Less integrity than integrated approach	

SSADM starts with an analysis of the performance, operation and problems associated with the current system, where such a system exists.

The purpose of this approach is to:

- allow the analysts to learn the terminology and functionality of the users' environment;

- provide for investigation of current data;

- introduce users to the techniques used within SSADM; and

- define limits for the project.

The rest of the process then attempts to evolve the system from the current design to the new requirements. There is an assumption made to justify this process that although processes may change, underlying data needs do not vary enormously.

This approach places the need to take account of existing systems as a very high priority. The criticism that is made is that the process does not encourage innovation and change, and lacks a strategic view.

The alternative class of methods includes Information Engineering and ORACLE's proprietary method, both of which emphasize strategy, coverage of the whole life cycle and integration. Their suppliers claim that integration with existing systems is feasible and that the systems may co-exist until the existing systems may be converted or replaced. Practitioners' experience suggests otherwise.

Within an integrated approach starting with the global information strategy, the analysis phase follows as a direct consequence of the strategic information plan. This encourages a more cohesive view of systems and is superficially more appealing. However, in practice, the existence of existing systems which may not fit the neat global picture can ruin the elegant cohesion (Fig. 10.1).

This has forced at least one organization to adopt an integrated CASE tool for their new projects where there is little or no computerization of the existing system, but, retain other more fragmented methods for those projects which must integrate with existing computer systems.

The failure of CASE method and tool vendors to agree on interchangeable standards for CASE is reminiscent of the old days of proprietary mainframes, when the major players such as IBM, DEC and ICL tried to tie customers in to their own systems.

Thus it would appear that integrated CASE tool vendors are attempting to establish sites where the whole of systems development is tied into their development methods and tools. This would appear to be an unwise commercial strategy as all sites will have existing systems and the current state of reverse engineering does not allow the existing systems to be easily transformed into a CASE-compatible form.

An organization with a substantial investment in existing integrated management information systems appears to have only two options at present, illustrated in Fig. 10.2.

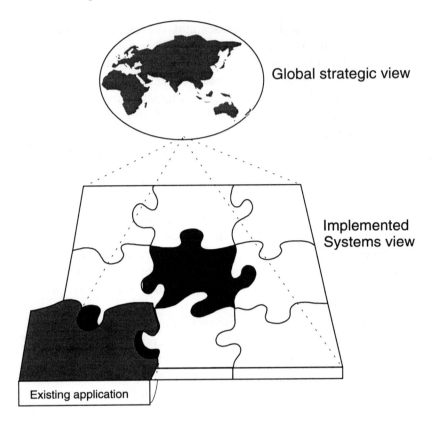

Fig. 10.1 Existing systems may not fit comfortably in a strategic view.

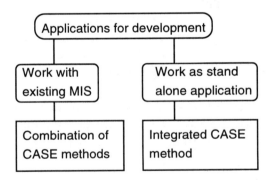

Fig. 10.2 Two-pronged approach.

Both of these represent partial solutions. These approaches are based upon the practice of a large company faced with these problems. They actually use both approaches in parallel.

10.1.1 Option 1: partial automation

In this strategy, the solution adopted is to apply CASE methods and tools to the first half of the life cycle. This can be achieved either through the front end of an integrated tool or the use of a front end tool itself.

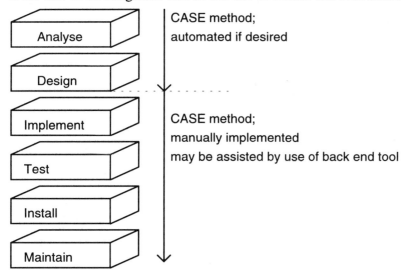

Fig. 10.3 Option 1: partial automation.

This leaves the latter part of the cycle to be carried out manually. In practice, this can be improved by the use of a back end CASE tool such as Telon. These tools will largely automate code generation but allow manual adaptation to incorporate facilities for integration with other applications. What is more important, they produce transparent and accessible code, unlike the code produced by most integrated tools which is incomprehensible to 'encourage' developers to use the tool the way that it was intended: as a complete package.

However, this fragmented use of tools does not provide the data integrity of an integrated approach. It also lacks the elegance of the theoretically integrated approach.

10.1.2 Option 2: Use integrated CASE where possible

To maximize the use of CASE the applications may be divided into those which are required to work with existing applications and those which are not. This allows those which are not required to be compatible with existing systems to be developed using a fully blown integrated CASE technique with the associated advantages of integration and integrity.

However, to run the two approaches in parallel involves much duplication, with two methods to learn, two sets of tools to buy and is an inelegant and expensive solution.

What the IT community has done in this case is to sell the business world the concept of integration with all its perceived advantages of data integrity, efficiency and elegance. However, in any organization where there are existing systems which need to be integrated with new applications, the current technology cannot deliver integration in both the development methods and tools and the final systems (Fig. 10.4)

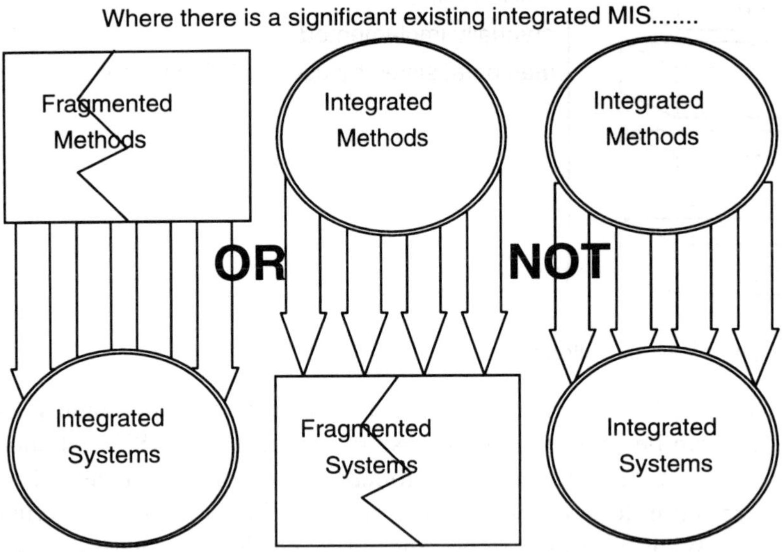

Where there is a significant existing integrated MIS.......

Fragmented Methods

Integrated Methods

Integrated Methods

OR   NOT

Integrated Systems

Fragmented Systems

Integrated Systems

Fig. 10.4 The problem with integration.

Although many of the case studies used in the book pre-date the time of writing (mid-1993), an informal telephone survey of CASE users suggests that this is still true.

The technologically centred solution to this problem is reverse engineering, which seeks to re-engineer the old systems, and therefore permit the use of integration in both development and implemented systems. How far this is possible will be examined next.

10.2   REVERSE ENGINEERING

The term 'software engineering' has been in use for some years now and there is a consensus that the term refers to a systematic process to move from a business problem to actual operational code.

However, in recent years the terms 're-engineering' and 'reverse engineering' have appeared on the scene. Being a much more immature technology, there is little consensus as to meaning. Some use re-engineering to describe the process of simply tidying up existing software. Others use the same term to describe the process of extracting business logic from existing systems; literally the reverse of software engineering. Therefore, others describe that second procedure by the term 'reverse engineering'. Unfortunately, others use that term to describe the complete cycle of business logic extraction followed by system rebuilding.

As well as the relative immaturity of the technology, there are those who would argue that there are people with vested interests who would oppose clarification. The process of integrating and maintaining existing systems within a fully blown integrated CASE development environment is dependent upon the ability to recreate those systems within the format of the CASE environment.

Reverse engineering is therefore not a luxury but a necessity for the effective working of such environments. It is perhaps easy to see what we would like from reverse engineering. Its aim has been stated as:

'To extract the contents, structure, and flow of data and processes contained within existing system software in a form amenable to inquiry, analysis and documentation.'

However, much remains to be done to realize the dream (Fig. 10.5) in its entirety.

The primary purpose of reverse engineering is thus to translate existing source code, whether in COBOL, PL/1 4GL or whatever, into a form which can be dealt with in the CASE environment, and therefore recreated in such a way that it can be maintained according to the evolving needs of the organization.

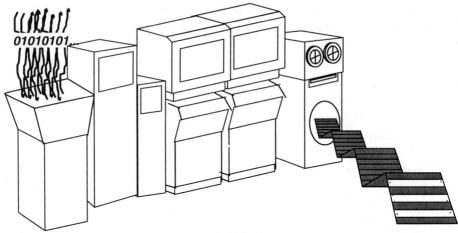

Fig. 10.5 Reverse engineering...the technologist's dream.

The importance of reverse engineering is that most code in use in organizations was written before the advent of the current methods and tools. Unless this code can be brought into the CASE fold, the benefits to the organization will be small for a long time to come.

At the last count, the United States alone spends $30 thousand million a year simply supporting old COBOL code. One estimate even goes so far as to indicate that total US spending on software maintenance amounts to no less than 2% of the country's total gross national product.

Furthermore, the problem is getting worse. The US Air Force, for example, recently announced that it costs between $2500 and $3000 to change just one line of application code. From this figure, it projected that, unless it could alter in some fundamental way the software maintenance equation, it would require 45% of the country's 18–25 year olds to maintain its software by the end of the century. Figures for the UK are equally grim. Durham University's Centre for Software Maintenance estimates that the UK spends more than £1 thousand million each year on maintaining software.

These figures will not be addressed by CASE for new systems alone; as systems get older, maintenance costs rise and this is likely to more than outweigh the reduced costs associated with newer systems developed under CASE.

There is a point in the evolution of every market where vendors feel the need to try to overcome customer indifference by the excessive use of hyperbole. Thus, five years ago early CASE marketeers forecast that their new tools would 'eliminate programming totally'. Today, a fair number of the hyperbole merchants appear to be in the reverse engineering market. There is much talk about using reverse engineering tools to 'reincarnate business logic souls from program cadavers', of the new 'top down/bottom up' approach to systems development, and even about the foolhardiness of attempting to build computer systems using the 'top down' approach to software development.

Reverse engineering is currently suffering from a level of hype previously reserved for the likes of artificial intelligence. The reality is somewhat different. At a practical level, no-one is yet able routinely to offer business logic reincarnation. Further, the methods available are not nearly as well developed as those of software engineering. The field is younger and the problem more complex.

It is likely, however, that reverse engineering will not go away, simply because of the commercial necessity to find a solution. Much work is currently underway and in the longer term it may prove more important than current ideas on forward systems engineering.

In the meantime we shall consider what the current generation of tools can do for us.

10.2.1 The current role of tools

Existing reverse engineering tools are designed to extract a limited amount of helpful information from current systems. Whilst they are not the promised code transmuters, they can assist software developers in the tasks of:

- documenting existing code

- cross referencing

- understanding how the code is organized.

They can function at the module, program, application, library or installation level. One of the most important observations is that although these tools may fall short of the unrealistic expectations set for them, they can still make a valuable contribution to productivity in maintaining existing systems.

An analogy may be made here with the field of artificial intelligence. The attempts to build intelligent machines, promised in the 1950s have failed in the eyes of most people. However, all over the world, small scale knowledge based systems are making meaningful contributions to their organizations. These systems are not 'intelligent' in any meaningful way and they may not produce the spectacular results promised; however, they are still making a useful and profitable contribution in many areas.

The tools to support these activities are known as software resource analysis tools. The case for them is that before a programmer can actually alter program code, they must spend much time working out which code to alter. Figures from IBM, for example, indicate that upwards of 50% of software maintenance is concerned with investigation and analysis. In a sense, what analysis tools offer is a method of building complex cross reference indices to the software resource.

Although the tools that fall into this category are technologically the simplest in reverse engineering terms, they are probably the most attractive to development staff in the short term.

Once this level of activity is working effectively, it is possible to make use of code restructuring tools to generate new source code. The commercial benefit of this is easy to see in reduced maintenance costs associated with well-structured code. This will then leave the organization well placed to take advantage of any further developments that come along.

Code restructuring tools which support this level of activity simply take spaghetti (i.e. unstructured) code in, and generate a new program in a structured form. The underlying business logic remains unaltered. The restructured program should be easier to maintain. There is, however, a 'down side' to restructuring. The tools are heavy in their use of machine resources. Source and object code sizes typically increase by between 10 and 20%. Run-time CPU increases can vary between 5 and 10%.

More worrying, perhaps, is the criticism that restructuring tools can devastate what has become a familiar program structure. Inevitably, restructuring alters irrevocably what are probably well-known program 'landmarks'. Whilst reasonably successful in the US, code restructuring has made little impact in Europe.

Just as it is those organizations who already have well-developed methods in place that benefit most from automation through CASE, so it is those organizations who have experience of the limited reverse engineering techniques and tools currently available who will be well placed to take advantage of future developments.

Those future developments are highly sought after but little in evidence. The Bachman tool, for reverse engineering definitions from

IMS and IDMS into DB2, perhaps the most successful, can currently only deal with data. Like CASE vendors before it, Bachman has recognized how much easier it is to deal with the data side of development than with the process side. However, what is happening on the data side is also being mirrored on the process side.

A number of organizations have products that abstract business logic from existing COBOL applications. Following this process of abstraction, developers are able to manipulate that logic at a 'design level', using it as the basis of software development and enhancement. Certainly, all the leading CASE vendors are working on tools designed to achieve exactly that.

The process of reverse engineering patently needs a target into which to abstract the essence of existing systems. This can then become a source from which to generate new systems. A CASE repository can fulfil both those functions.

A repository for reverse engineering shares many of the properties of current repositories for forward engineering. The principal requirement is for flexibility; traditional 'data processing' databases are not flexible enough to represent meaningfully the subtlety and complexity of the models needed to support systems development and maintenance.

Current developments are based around object-oriented or entity-relationship models. There is, however, a gap between the current achievements and the actual requirements.

10.2.2 Current limitations

The dream of true reverse engineering in the sense of automatic regeneration of existing spaghetti code systems into nice neatly structured systems remains a dream, at least for the present.

It is, however, possible to set up a reverse engineering method which makes use of the current generation of tools. The role of tools in this process should be viewed as assisting in the process of rebuilding systems rather than automating the process. Again we may use the analogy of artificial intelligence.

We would like to have truly automatic reverse engineering tools, just as we would like to have truly intelligent systems for automating decision making processes. In practice we have a range of tools which are analogous to decision support and information processing systems, which, whilst they are not what we might ideally want, can make a useful contribution.

Furthermore, it has been shown in AI that there are both advantages to human control of the process and disadvantages to full automation. Human control of the process allows user involvement in the reconstruction process. It is almost certain that old systems need adaptation to current business needs.

The process of testing and validation is easier when humans control the process as well. Therefore, a headlong rush to complete automation may not provide the best business solution anyway.

The current tools do permit an evolutionary approach to the problem of reverse engineering, from the use of simple tools to document and record the structure of existing systems through to tools which go some way towards the dream of automatic system generation.

The evolutionary approach minimizes risk and change, which is particularly important in a field which is very immature. Although CASE is a relatively new technology, it has its roots in ideas established and accepted for twenty years. Compared to this, reverse engineering in all its forms is practically brand new. As with all new technologies, it is likely to be characterized by unrealistic expectations, exaggerated claims and changes of direction for some time to come.

The smart approach is to stay just behind the state of the art, adopting the underlying principles of the process with the minimum investment in high risk areas which may turn out to be blind alleys. As with forward software engineering, it is the principles and methods which should be established first. These will bring many benefits, particularly when used in conjunction with basic tools. The more glamorous excursions into large expensive tools are likely to bring less return at higher risk and it is hard to see the justification at this stage in business terms.

Table 10.2 The analogy with AI

	Decision making	*Reverse engineering*
	Intelligent systems	Fully automated system regeneration tools
	Decision support systems	Code restructuring tools
	Information processing and storage systems	CASE repositories

For the future, the reverse engineering bandwagon is rolling and the commercial imperative is likely to drive it forward. It is already possible to foresee the emergence of a whole new approach to software development that takes the best of both top down and reverse engineering approaches. Future methodologies will emphasize the need to develop software as business evolves. However, the problem of tidying up current applications is undoubtedly here for many years to come.

It will be necessary to use the top down approach to establish the correct information architecture to support future developments and to continue to use business-oriented methods of analysis. However, for the next decade, there will be a process of abstracting from existing systems the logic needed to build conceptual models of existing operational computer systems.

Gradually, the top down and bottom up models will be combined to produce 'super-models' that reflect day to day business reality. Once the super-models are in place, software developers will continue to use a combination of techniques to enhance them in response to business changes. However, all development or enhancement work will take place at the design level, not at the code level.

Reverse engineering consists of understanding those parts of an existing system at the physical design level. It is useful if it is carried out for those systems or system components which will play a direct part in the parallel running of a new system. Reverse engineering is a highly skilled, manpower-intensive exercise to make sense of the amount of available and accessible information in a real-world system. Some computer assistance is available to help translate the machine readable components of the computer portion of systems. These products are code and data structure reformatters: they do not fundamentally change the knowledge about a system. Such reformatting is useful and necessary where it can be used to design new systems coherently. To operate reverse engineering, possibly partially automated, as part of a top-down development discipline, in conjunction with other techniques, is a pragmatic addition to software development.

10.3 CASE STUDY

10.3.1 The company: almost a green field site

The company has a turnover of over £10M and it employs 100 people. It is part of a larger group with a total turnover of £120M The company typically produces over 200 orders per day with many of them having a value of less than £100. It produces bias bindings, trouser waistbands, hook and eye tape, pocketing, braided, knitted and woven elastics, tapes and webbing and. It does not hold much finished stock but can, if required, make and deliver within 24 hours. Its order book normally covers about six weeks' production.

When a new managing director arrived in 1981, the company's practices had changed very little from when the company was set up in

1938. The problem was that the initial processing of the orders, more than 100 per day, was taking too long. The pricing of the orders was very complicated and time consuming. The price is dependent on the type of cloth, cloth width, folding, stitching, gluing, packing, etc. Orders were just not getting onto and off the factory floor quickly enough. Invoices and statements were not sent out quickly enough and cash flow was a problem. The solution was to computerize the production of works orders, invoices and delivery notes, using bespoke software, and buy off-the-shelf accounts and payroll packages. Extra production machines were put into the factory so that production could react quickly to customer requirements. Workers in the factory are able to operate on a number of different machines.

The clerical procedures were very good but slow and cumbersome and had allowed the building of 'empires' by individuals who were reluctant to change. The computer system modelled the clerical procedures and was put in against resistance from the existing staff. The number of staff doing the clerical work has been reduced from 10 to 3. Most staff have been redeployed. The clerical tasks have been de-skilled but staff are now multi-skilled. The company now processes over 200 orders per day. The system provides a wide variety of senior management reports which allow the efficient control of the company.

The computer systems have made the company more profitable. Once the company had sorted out its internal workings it allowed the directors time to look at the long term future of the business. The company has grown by acquiring five companies with turnovers in the £2M to £3.5M range. The computer systems have been installed in some of these companies. This growth by acquisition has been achieved with an increase of only one person in the administration section.

In November 1988, a disgruntled employee started a fire which destroyed the complete factory, stocks, orders, etc. The director had taken home back-up copies of the system and data. A program was generated which listed the outstanding order position and important customer orders. Critical production was moved to another factory in the group and the rest of the orders were contracted out to other manufacturers. Production was re-started within a week. The computer system kept track of all orders and their location. The company would not have survived without the back-up program and data copies. As a result of the fire all the manual purchase ordering data was lost. The directors considered that the time was ripe to implement a purchase ordering system. Thus the fire actually provided the almost mythical green field site that CASE tools are ideally suited to.

10.3.2 Conclusions

All systems have been developed using software engineering methods and tools. The use of such techniques, together with the use of effective backup procedures at a time of crisis, has enabled the business to develop information systems which meet their needs effectively.

This case provides as near a green field site as one is ever likely to meet. In the first instance, procedures and systems had changed little in fifty years and were largely manual in nature. The fire further reduced the level of existing systems and thus enabled further systems to be added according to a clear strategic plan. This has enabled the company to introduce their new development procedures and resulting computer systems with minimum fuss and to maximum effect.

However, even such a green field site has an existing information system and culture. The information system may be paper based and the culture old-fashioned, but it should not be ignored. In situations where the existing systems are already computerized, then the issue of back compatibility is often more complex.

10.4 SUMMARY

In this chapter we have explored the problem of integrating and maintaining existing systems within an integrated CASE environment. We have identified the problems and proposed a range of solutions from those involving changing working practices to those which require the introduction of more technology.

In this context we have explored the development of reverse engineering tools and tried to separate the truth from the hype. The key points of this chapter are:

- CASE can only address escalating maintenance costs by dealing with the problem of existing systems.

- Existing methods and tools do not easily allow integration of new and existing systems.

- The technology of reverse engineering is a long way from maturity.

• Current reverse engineering tools can help in the restructuring of existing systems.

FURTHER READING

Choi, S.C. and Scacchi, W. (1991) SOFTMAN: environment for forward and reverse CASE *Information and Software Technology*, **33**(9), 664–674.

Kozaczynski, W., Liongosari, E.S. and Ning, J.Q. (1991) BAL/SRW: Assembler re-engineering workbench. *Information and Software Technology*, **33**(9), 675–684.

These papers describe two approaches to the problem of reverse engineering.

11

Serving the business needs

11.1 THE IT CULTURE GAP

In the 1960s, the software crisis was identified as the problem of managing increasing system complexity. In the 1990s, there is a new crisis arising from the fact that users regard many of the systems provided for them as inappropriate and failing to meet their needs. The authors have already suggested that much of the maintenance effort is in fact spent upon making systems fit user needs better rather than correcting errors in coding.

This is reflected in a lack of confidence in the ability of the IT community to deliver the systems that people want. This is precisely the kind of problem that CASE should be able to address. However, should CASE fail to deliver, then this will reinforce the current scepticism.

This scepticism is increasing at board and chief executive level regarding large-scale IT projects in general. Price Waterhouse (1990, 1992) have identified this in a study of director attitudes to IT. They identify the underlying problem as a 'culture gap' between business people and the IT professionals. They asked IT directors to identify the symptoms and effects of this culture gap. The symptoms identified in order of priority were:

- IT potential not appreciated by top management;

- Business implications of IT not appreciated by IT staff;

- Business people have difficulty integrating IT people into the organization;

- Business people don't trust IT people;

- Differences between centralization of business and IT not appreciated;

- Powerful departments pursue local interest at expense of integration;

- Power is separated from responsibility.

The effects identified in the Price Waterhouse studies were:

- Loss of IT opportunities;

- Forcing justification of IT investment by artificial measurement of intangibles;

- Putting in the wrong, or ill-conceived, systems;

- Adding burden to IT management whilst not harming company performance;

- Over-concentration on cheap solutions and cost cutting;

- Denying opportunity for brainstorming with top executives;

- Jeopardising future of company by failure to install core systems.

If this culture gap is perceived within an organization then the worst thing that can be undertaken is a large scale investment in further technology in the face of board scepticism. In such a situation, the symptoms are often identified as poor service from the IT function. Their response can be to throw themselves into ever more sophisticated technological solutions to address the symptoms. This will merely dig themselves deeper into the mire.

Instead, a fundamental review of roles and functions is required before any further large scale IT projects can be undertaken. The correct order of events in such a scenario is first sort out the management issues, then the fundamental working practices of the IT section. Then and only then should those working practices be automated using a CASE tool.

Unless there is sound management and practice already, then adding a tool will simply add complexity and confusion. There is increasing evidence (Lehman, 1990) that those organizations who are successfully implementing CASE tools already have a sound base of working methods on which to build.

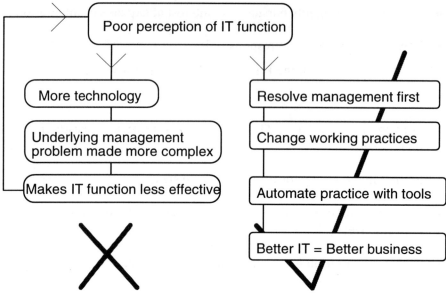

Fig. 11.1 A wrong and a right strategy.

Thus, organizations with the greatest need for CASE methods and tools may not be best placed to gain the benefits sought by senior management. By contrast, those organizations with well-managed IT functions with good existing practice and a good understanding of the business of their customers, whether internal or external, will draw the greatest benefits.

The starting point for breaking down any 'culture gap' which may exist is to establish clear aims and objectives for both business and IT and to ensure that all parties are clear how the IT objectives support the business objectives.

Having established where the business is going and where IT must go to support it, the next stage is to establish a strategy to get there. In an ideal world, the IT strategy will be part of an overall business strategy. However, in many organizations this will be a somewhat Utopian ideal. Where the IT strategy is separate from the business strategy, each component of the IT strategy must be measured against the criterion of what part of the business strategy does it serve?

11.2 THE IT STRATEGY

It is possible to use software engineering effectively yet still have no IT strategy. So why bother? Without a suitable strategy, the wrong systems may be produced, albeit efficiently and to a high technical quality. The benefit to the business of such systems is likely to be limited.

The IT strategy sits between the business strategy and the software development strategy. The latter is likely to have been produced by the DP department and will make statements about how it is intended to develop systems. This may include details of the hardware environment, the software environment, methods of working, level of support, development time scales and so on.

The business strategy is a top-down statement, while the development strategy tends to be bottom-up. It attempts to tackle the IT problems within the organization. The development strategy may solve many of the operational problems faced by the business, but there is no guarantee that the software solutions produced will be those best placed to meet the business needs of the organizations.

The missing link is an IT strategy. The purpose of such a strategy is threefold: to ensure that the systems developed are the ones required, to ensure that the systems meet real business needs and finally to set priorities. Priorities are required to prevent reaction to crisis, reaction to who 'shouts the loudest' and reaction to who has the most 'muscle' in the organization.

The IT strategy is a plan of what the organization wants to achieve with its IT systems and how it is going to achieve it. The business objectives and needs are of prime importance when formulating the strategy. It is the responsibility of top management and not the responsibility of computer specialists, although management will need help and guidance from senior computer professionals whilst formulating the strategy.

An IT strategy should anticipate future developments in the business, such as changing business needs, the ability to finance software developments and new methods of working. In addition, it should foster an appreciation of good practice, consider the implications of other management issues and determine how IT can give the organization a competitive edge.

To complement the top-down approach, there needs to be bottom up planning. This area, in particular, is where there can be a valuable input from the senior computer professionals in the organization. The bottom-up approach should consider the ways in which new technology can create opportunities, the strengths and weaknesses in current systems, future threats from competition, technical constraints and statutory changes.

At a detailed level, the IT strategy should define a framework for software development. This consists of the four stages described below.

11.2.1 The life-cycle model

The IT strategy should define the phases of the life-cycle to be used by the organization. The baselines, objectives and outputs of each phase should be clearly stated. It is necessary to define the interfaces between phases to ensure that there are no overlaps or omissions between them. The validation and verification procedures and the quality control procedures must also be clearly defined at this stage.

11.2.2 Standards and procedures

The standards and procedures to be used by the organization need to be specified. These should include a statement on the content and quality of all internal and user documentation. The quality assurance procedures need to be specified together with the quality management system. The procedures for project management and control should also be detailed.

11.2.3 Methods

When the life cycle model, standards and procedures, quality control, quality assurance and project management procedures have been specified, it is then possible to select the method(s) to be used. It is important that methods are selected after the procedures are put in place, not before.

11.2.4 Tools

Software tools can be used to support development methods and other software engineering activities. Tools help to automate the software development processes, but they are ineffective without the underlying standards, procedures and methods. They should only be selected after the earlier phases of the framework are in place.

Once the IT strategy has been completed, it should be thoroughly documented. It should be updated each year to identify existing and unforeseen IT requirements, to specify how these are to be met and to specify procedures to establish priorities amongst these projects.

11.3 CASE AND THE IT STRATEGY

The link between the CASE methods and tools adopted and the IT strategy will depend upon the mode of implementation. Where the full integrated CASE approach is used then the IT strategy is the result of the first stage of the integrated life cycle.

ORACLE (Barker, 1990), in their integrated method, describe the resulting strategy as a complete but not detailed analysis from which a broad based business model can be built. They suggest that the key deliverables which make up the strategy are:

- statement of business direction

- top level entity relationship model

- function hierarchy

- recommendations

- organizational, technological or other issues

- definition of the system boundary

- possible system architecture

- phased development plan

- resource statement.

This somewhat daunting list of deliverables is to be built up by interviewing the key executives in the organization. The model is then built and refined in consultation with the same people. The process proposed is illustrated in Fig. 11.2.

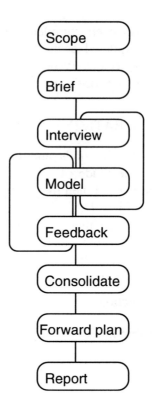

Fig. 11.2 The ORACLE approach to deriving an information strategy.

This approach has been used by ORACLE themselves with their clients. However, as a more general approach, it does have a number of disadvantages. The principal disadvantage is its complexity.

The conventional solution to this problem is to use consultants to assist in the process of drawing up the IT strategy. This suffers from two problems:

- The first problem is cost. Consultants are expensive, and an IT strategy can take many consultant-days.

- The second problem is the problem of external people playing a major part in deriving the strategy. They cannot have the same in-depth knowledge of the business as an internal manager and the resulting strategy may not be adopted enthusiastically if it is perceived as the invention of outsiders. For the consultants to play a genuine enabling role, giving the company managers the knowledge to draw up their own strategy, will be even more expensive than if the consultants do much of the work themselves.

It is therefore suggested that the process of deriving an IT strategy should be a simpler one. The following process is suggested:

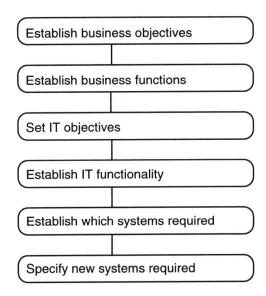

Fig 11.3 Simplified generic route to an IT strategy.

This approach may be considered in six stages. The first is the establishment of business objectives. These should already be in existence, in the business strategy document or business plan. From these objectives, it is necessary to derive the required business functionality necessary to achieve these objectives.

Each of these business functions may then be supported (or hindered) by IT provision. First it is necessary to establish IT objectives in terms of which business functions may best be supported and how. Once the IT objectives are established, then the necessary functionality may be defined for the systems needed to meet the objectives set.

Finally, each system must be specified in terms of a preliminary specification, including scope, size, estimated cost and time for development, to provide enough information so that a business case may be made for each proposed system to ensure that its benefits outweigh its cost.

This approach does not differ radically from proprietary approaches, but does offer a number of significant simplifications to the uninitiated.

First, the strategy should be drawn up by a small working group who represent both business and IT functions and different levels of the management hierarchy. This is essential if the strategy is to be accepted and 'owned' by all parties. The group's size should be about half a dozen: smaller and it runs the risk of not representing all interests; too big and it becomes a committee.

Secondly, the outputs should avoid the use of specialized diagramming techniques. At the level of detail required, they offer little benefit and serve only to confuse the uninitiated. Simple tree diagrams should suffice to display the information required in the strategy output documents.

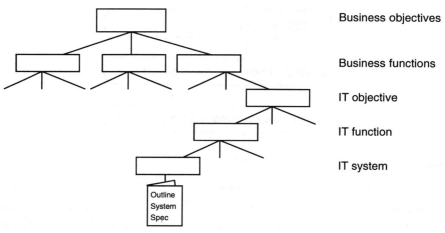

Fig 11.4 Output representation of IT strategy.

The crucial level of detail which must not be omitted is the links between each part of the process. Thus it should be clearly established which business function follows from which objective, which IT objective supports that business function, which IT function supports which IT objective, and which systems are required to deliver that IT function.

In this way, it is possible to establish an 'audit trail' through the strategy so that the need for each system is traceable back to a specific business objective and function. This then allows informed decisions to be made as to the business case for a particular system.

11.4 PROVIDING A BETTER SERVICE

The impact of CASE tools and methods upon the quality of information systems is generally assessed in terms of technical criteria for the quality. Most of these may be traced back to a classical model of McCall (1977) established in the late 1970s. His criteria were: correctness, reliability, efficiency, integrity, usability, maintainability, flexibility, testability, portability, re-usability and interoperability. There are a number of problems with these criteria in a business context.

First, they are a necessary but not complete set. This means that it is probably necessary for a system to meet all McCall's criteria to be a successful business application, but it is perfectly possible to meet these criteria and provide a system which is unacceptable to the people who are to use it.

Secondly, although they highlight areas where problems may arise, they do not identify where in the software process those problems are caused.

Finally, they focus upon the quality of systems, rather than the quality of the service provided by the IT function. Where IT is an internal function, it is a supplier of a support service in the eye of the rest of the business, rather than a product vendor. Even where the customer is external, and software is sold as a product, the business case for spending the money will be made in terms of the effect that the software has upon the overall effectiveness of the business. The software supplier is still providing a service to the business in the same way and the ultimate test of the software remains, how does it impact upon the business as a whole.

In a regional survey of large companies in the north west of England (Gillies, 1993) the companies identified symptoms similar to those described in the Price Waterhouse studies (1990,1992). A consistent theme was that the IT function and the systems provided did not meet the needs of users. When this was examined further, the companies highlighted a series of problems which are not simply about the technical quality of systems but rather relate to the quality of the service provided by the IT function.

The problems raised by business users included:

- A lack of support from the IT function.

- User dissatisfaction with the system once working.

- Difficulties in transition from an old system to a new one.

- Failure to deliver in order to meet business deadlines.

- Failure to consult users.

- Inaccurate results.

- Failure to appreciate the time required to complete a task in use.

- Systems that people didn't actually like.

- Inflexible systems.

- Failure to meet the cost/benefit objectives.

- Systems unsympathetic to human ways of working (Fig. 11.5).

Fig. 11.5 Users find systems unsympathetic to their way of working.

To consider the impact of CASE upon these problems we must first consider the likely underlying factors which are the cause of the symptoms described. These are considered in Table 11.1.

Table 11.1 Reported and underlying problems

Reported problem	Possible underlying problems
A lack of support from IT staff	• Poor relationship between IT and business staff
User dissatisfaction with the system once working	• Poor communication during analysis
	• Poor implementation leading to unreliability, inefficiency
Difficulties in transition from an old system to a new one	• Lack of planning and strategy
	• Failure to appreciate users' problems
	• Inflexible tool prevents integration
Failure to deliver in order to meet business deadlines	• Poor productivity
	• Poor estimation
	• Failure to appreciate customer needs
Failure to consult users	• Poor relationship between IT and business staff
Inaccurate results	• Poor design
	• Poor testing
	• Poor integrity
Failure to appreciate the time needed to complete a task in use	• Poor analysis
	• Poor communication
Systems that people didn't like	• Poor relationship between IT and business staff
Inflexible systems	• Poor design leading to unstructured code with low maintainability
Failure to meet the cost/benefit objectives	• Poor analysis leading to low benefit
	• Poor productivity leading to high cost
Systems unsympathetic to human ways of working	• Poor analysis
	• Poor relationship between IT and business staff

The table shows that the underlying problems may be classified as problems with development methods and cultural problems in the organization. Generally, the use of CASE methods will have a positive impact in the area of problems arising from poor development methods. Therefore they could be expected to address the issues arising from them.

For example, the cost and difficulty of development and maintenance is at the root of problems in timeliness of delivery and flexibility in the face of changing business needs. CASE methods and tools should also reduce the problem of inaccurate results by assisting in the detection and correction of errors. Systems based upon structured methods are more maintainable and adaptable and should therefore prove more flexible in the face of changing business needs.

Finally, better analysis and design methods should improve estimation of costs and the reliability of such estimates by providing a more consistent environment for system development. Better analysis may help with the clarity of the system objectives, and therefore lead to a better appreciation of the benefits or perhaps lack of them.

These factors taken together should improve the probability of a system meeting its cost/benefit objectives.

However, a number of caveats must be sounded. The first is that none of these benefits will come immediately and indeed performance in some of these areas is likely to suffer in the short term. It is therefore essential that customers of the IT department understand the implications and motivation for adopting CASE methods and tools.

Secondly, we have already seen that the impact of CASE methods and tools is not necessarily universally beneficial even when considering solely the development process and its associated problems. The impact of CASE tools may be considered for McCall's criteria.

Table 11.2 considers the impact of CASE upon each criterion at three stages of implementation: initially, then at steady state and finally in the best possible case where the CASE technology delivers all that is promised. The impact is expressed in terms of the following classification system:

✓✓	Strongly beneficial
✓	Beneficial
O	Neutral or application dependent
×	Detrimental
××	Strongly detrimental

Table 11.2 The effect of CASE upon McCall's criteria

Criteria	Impact			Comments
	Initial	Steady	Best	
Correctness	✓	✓✓	✓✓	Some benefit initially.
				Greater benefit with experience.
Reliability	O	✓✓	✓✓	At start, some gains but some losses with errors arising from inexperience.
				As experience grows, so gains retained but losses reduced.
Efficiency	××	××	×	Structured code is always less efficient.
				Generated code appears worse.
Integrity	O	✓✓	✓✓	Comments as for reliability.
Usability	O	✓	✓	Benefits arise from use of rapid prototyping tools.
Maintainability	✓	✓✓	✓✓	Structured methods will produce benefits; more with experience.
Flexibility	O	✓	✓✓	Compatibility problems with existing systems reduce benefit at start.
				Structured methods will produce benefits; more with experience.
Testability	✓	✓✓	✓✓	Comments as for maintainability
Portability	××	××	O	Fully integrated CASE tools reduce external compatibility unless whole establishment is CASE built.
Re-usability	××	××	O	Fully integrated CASE tools reduce re-usability unless whole establishment is CASE built.
Interoperability	××	××	O	Comments as for portability.

The other factor associated with the development process itself is productivity. We have already seen how productivity will at first decrease and then improve with experience. This should have a positive impact in the medium to long term upon the issues of the failure to deliver to meet business deadlines and high costs arising from poor productivity.

Thus the ability of CASE to impact upon the issues highlighted by users is much stronger in the medium to long term than it is in the short term.

Further, it must be recognized that CASE tools and methods cannot in themselves change attitudes and cultures. Therefore, CASE alone is likely to affect only slightly those factors arising from cultural and organizational issues.

There are procedures published for the breaking down of the culture gap, e.g. LOQUM (Gillies,1993) but such techniques are not generally part of the CASE approach. However, used sensitively and effectively, CASE methods and tools can facilitate user–developer communication, particularly with rapid prototyping tools to demonstrate 'look and feel' to users.

To provide a solution for these issues it is necessary to see CASE as part of a broader process of improvement which will be discussed in the next chapter. In the longer term, customers will judge the effectiveness of the new methods and tools by the quality of the service and systems that the IT function provides, and it is simply not enough to focus solely upon the development process.

11.5   CASE STUDY

11.5.1 The company

The company is part of a group of companies operating throughout the UK and Western Europe, providing a range of marketing services which include tele-marketing, direct mail, campaign design, training and consultancy. The company was formed in 1984 with the aim of building a database of the major computer sites in the UK and using this to provide marketing support to the IT industry. The expertise acquired in building this database is now being transferred, through consultancy, to their clients, many of whom are building their own databases and the turnover of the company has reached approximately £2M.

As far as computers are concerned, networked Datapoint micros were replaced by an IBM System/38 in 1986 and Apple Macintoshes are also widely used as personal workstations. Generally the attitude of management is to understand the benefits of IT but to be sceptical about the possibility of these benefits being realized in practice. IT 'experts' are seen as generally unreliable, often giving conflicting advice and rarely being willing to be held accountable for their recommendations. They are perceived as being too willing to blame circumstances and find reasons for things not working out as planned.

11.5.2 The information business environment

The company is in the business of marketing and there are many apparent parallels between marketing and IT. Both are essentially simple to understand and benefit from, and yet both tend to be misunderstood, misused and blamed for failures, to the detriment of the organizations of which they are a part. Above all else success in marketing depends upon teamwork. It requires a fusion of the communication skills of telephone marketeers to collect up-to-date and accurate information, the technical skills of DP to provide the systems which can hold and process this information, the academic skills of statisticians to describe markets with mathematical models and the talents of copywriters and graphic designers to create the marketing message.

The raw material of marketing is information. The idea of information as a resource is relatively new and generally not well understood. It would be a very radical organization that tomorrow morning instructs its sales force that their primary objective is no longer to close sales but is, instead, to collect information, and that from now on commission will be paid according to the amount and quality of information they collect, and yet ideas like this are already being discussed quite seriously. Therefore, in data processing, we are dealing with people who understand the commercial value of information very well, and who look to us to provide the tools to process it.

11.5.3 The project

At the beginning of 1987, the company had a problem. They had a maintenance backlog as the result of new methods of research and new areas of interest that had to be incorporated into their computer systems.

They were faced with a growing DP department and a growing DP bill. Their clients were facing longer and longer lead times before changing needs could be met. Product was being delivered late. At the same time, the company were being successful, demand for their products was growing and management wanted to expand the company, particularly into new European markets. DP was becoming the major limiting factor to growth. What the DP function wanted to do was redesign the database, but this meant re-writing most of the applications software, which was estimated to be a twelve-month project.

The project objectives were stated as follows:

- to redesign the database;

- to rewrite the applications software;

- to allow for future changes in the database;

- to increase user involvement in the system;

- to allow for interfaces with other systems.

Technically this was feasible, but the problem was how to achieve the objectives within the available time. The system was to include four components, providing database definition, on-line update, report generation, PC and remote (Kilostream) links. A 4th generation language, Genesis V, was chosen as the major software tool in the development programme.

Within the old database, the primary unit of interest was some basic information about a company (name, address, etc.) which was held in a 'root' module. Linked to this would be a name file holding the details of people working for the company and various product files containing details of products used by the company, e.g. computers, company cars, etc. This information was arranged in a hierarchical structure. Adding a new product type or a new field to an existing product type involved changing the database, application programs and reports.

By contrast, the new database is based upon the relational model, with the root information and names held as separate tables. All product information is held in one table which contains a question code and an answer code (the answer text field allows for which may not be coded). Adding a new product type or a new field to an existing product type now involves no more than updating the question code table and the answer code table. This task may be carried out easily by the end user.

During the design stage, the company were also learning to use the tool and worked very closely with the supplier in an attempt to speed this process up. The system went live on the 1st January 1988. There was an increased (and unexpected) effort expended immediately after implementation. This was not due to any failure of the system but rather a result of a series of user initiated enhancements that taught the system developers a lot about design. The tool coped well with these changes.

11.5.4 Conclusions

The project was considered a success for a number of reasons. First, the reduced development time for the project enabled the company to meet the required deadlines for the development of the European products. In addition, the maintenance 'problem' was dramatically reduced. The end users took over responsibility for the systems and have been doing their own enhancements for a number of years. The system administrator is available for technical problems but now spends part of his time working for the clients and, incidentally, earning consultancy revenue for the company.

Perhaps the best indicator of success is, however, a strong feeling amongst the staff at the company that there is 'no going back' to the old methods.

11.6 SUMMARY

In this chapter we have considered the evidence for a culture gap between the IT function and the other business functions within an organization. We have considered the implications for CASE: the reluctance to invest, the need to meet business objectives as well as IT objectives, the need for a clear strategy providing a coherent IT function serving business needs.

Having considered the relationship between IT and the rest of the business at a strategic level we have then gone on to consider the implications for CASE at the operational level. We have stressed the need to see IT as a service and not a set of products. We have considered user concerns about their systems and considered how CASE can help address these concerns.

The key lessons from this chapter are:

- Information technology is a service function.

- There is much evidence for a culture gap between IT and business staff.

- Many issues are a product of the organizational culture rather than the development methods.

These issues cannot be addressed by CASE alone, but only as part of a coherent improvement programme. This topic will be considered in the next chapter.

FURTHER READING

Barker, R. (1990) *CASE Method: Tasks and Deliverables*, Addison-Wesley, Wokingham.

This book is the definitive guide to the ORACLE CASE method and includes information about their approach to deriving an IT strategy.

Price Waterhouse (1992) *Information Technology Review 1991/92*, Publications Office, Price Waterhouse, 32 Bridge Street, London, SE1 9SY, p. 7.

This report provides more information about the survey of IT directors from the 500 top UK companies, in which the IT 'culture gap' was identified

Gillies, A.C. (1992), Modelling software quality in the commercial environment. *Software Quality Journal*, **1** (3), 175–191

This paper describes the method and findings of the authors' regional study of quality practice in the north west of England. They identify many of the issues raised in this chapter.

12

CASE is just part of the process

12.1 CASE AND THE PROCESS OF PRODUCING SOFTWARE

The last chapter has shown how the ultimate purpose of information systems is to support the business objectives of an organization. If this purpose is to be realized then the process of producing software goes far beyond ensuring that the software is technically correct. It involves:

- recognition that IT has a service function;

- clarification of the overall process from business need to business solution;

- acceptance that software engineering is at the heart of the IT supply process, but dependent upon the processes which surround it (Fig. 12.1);

Fig. 12.1 Software engineering is at the heart of the IT supply process.

- recognition that the overall process is as strong as its weakest link;

- a commitment to continuous improvement of all processes.

The practical realization of this may be seen in the application of continuous improvement techniques, often referred to as Total Quality Management (TQM). These techniques generally lead to the establishment of a quality system. In the software context, one would expect a software engineering method to be at the heart of such a system, and it is a requirement of the ISO standard for such systems that a recognized systematic development method be employed.

In this chapter, we shall consider the use of these techniques and the impact of standards in the area of software development.

12.2   THE USE OF CONTINUOUS IMPROVEMENT TECHNIQUES IN SOFTWARE

Much has been written on the Japanese industrial miracle and how it is dependent upon the use of techniques to build quality into a process, rather than depend upon inspection at the end of the process. TQM techniques have been applied in many disciplines, well beyond the original application in manufacturing. Readers wishing to learn more are referred to the works of the gurus in the field, e.g. Deming (1986), Juran (1979) and Crosby (1986). Alternatively, more eclectic treatments are provided by Oakland (1989) and Gillies (1992b).

There is a backlash currently being witnessed in some quarters. TQM is currently very fashionable and this inevitably leads to a scepticism amongst those who have seen other fashions come and go. Many articles on the subject reinforce the view that the 'gurus' are treated with uncritical respect and this further undermines confidence in the sound underlying principles. In the context of software development, the basic principles may be established as:

- define the process

- document the process

- improve the process.

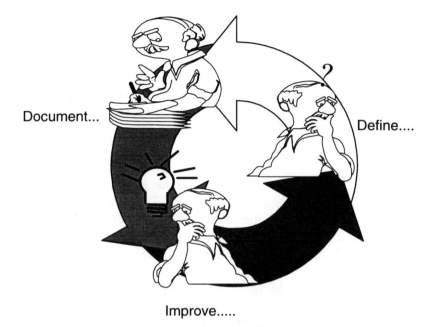

Document...   Define....

Improve.....

Fig. 12.2 Continuous improvement cycle.

This may be seen to have much in common with the application of software engineering methods and tools, which provide a systematic approach to software development. The application of ideas from quality management may be viewed as an extension of software engineering, expanding the scope in two critical ways:

- All related activity is deemed to be part of the process, including planning, estimation, project management and many other activities which are not generally included under the heading of 'software engineering', but affect the fitness of the IT function to perform its role in supporting business objectives.

- The systematic process is evolutionary: it should be constantly monitored, evaluated and improved.

The overall process is documented as a quality management system (QMS). The International Standards Organization (ISO, 1986) defines a quality management system as:

'The organizational structure, responsibilities, procedures, processes and resources for implementing quality management.'

The key to a successful implementation is a QMS that is a living system rather than a document gathering dust on a shelf. This may be achieved through the three stages illustrated in Fig. 12.2.

12.2.1 Define a systematic process

The definition of the process may be seen as an extension of the application of a software engineering method. Thus this view of the process includes all related activities: communication between users and developers, all aspects of project estimation, planning and management, as well as the underlying method to be applied to the engineering process itself.

It is often harder to achieve than the application of a software engineering method since it requires the imposition of structure and system on relatively unstructured tasks. The scope of a typical quality management system for software development will include, but not necessarily be restricted to, those described in Table 12.1.

12.2.2 Document the process

The manner of documentation of the process is crucial to the successful implementation of the overall improvement programme. The principal qualities of an effective document are clarity and usefulness. Most people stress thoroughness, but documents should only be as thorough as is useful and necessary. Documents that are too thorough will simply not be used as they will be too unwieldy. Obviously, however, there is a need for a sufficient level of detail.

The procedures described must be systematic in themselves and arranged in a systematic framework. Diagrams are nearly always preferable to words as they can communicate more information in a shorter time.

Table 12.1 Scope of a typical QMS for software development (after Taylor, 1989)

Requirement Procedures	Explanation
Review of operational requirements	An operational requirements specification is prepared. This will cover size, scope, multi-functionality, operational functions, implementation details, modularity and the tools, techniques and methods.
Design and development planning	A phased project management plan is prepared to cover the work and resources required. A quality control plan will also be developed. Plans will be drawn up for the acquisition of all resources, together with methods to identify, record and correct non-conformances.
Organization	The management structure for the project will be identified and recorded. Responsibility will be clearly identified for all aspects of quality control and quality assurance. A representative will be appointed to resolve quality matters to the satisfaction of the customer.
Training	Training will be provided for all new personnel working on the project in the matters of software development and quality assurance techniques. It will be ensured that all personnel have the required academic expertise and level of knowledge to fulfil their role.
Quality program	A quality program will be prepared and documented. The program document will include graphical descriptions of the work to be carried out, testing plans, documentation of the occurrences of non-conformance together with corrective action and definitions of the points at which each component can undergo formal qualification testing.
Management visibility and control	Methods and tools will be employed which positively encourage quality, particularly a formal ISD development methodology.
Design and development reviews	Reviews will be planned at the end of each development phase. The review should be carried out by independent staff, and open to scrutiny by the customer or an external body. Review documentation will include objectives, personnel functions, scope, provision for analysis and recommendations and procedures for verification of corrective actions.

Table 12.1 *cont'd*

Documentation	Documentation shall include the OR specification, planning and design documentation, the coded program and QA documentation
Support tools, techniques and methods	The tools and methods used should be identified, documented and validated.
Nonconformity, prevention and corrective action	Non-conformities should be eliminated as far as possible through the use of reviews and where necessary re-reviews at each stage.
Configuration control	Procedures should be drawn up to identify modules or programs, keep master versions secure, provide validated copies, obtain approval for modifications, ensure modifications are integrated, software media is properly marked, handled, and that non-conforming software is kept rigorously separated.
Subcontractor control	Procedures should be set up to ensure the quality of all subcontractor procedures, tools, methods and products and to delineate responsibility for the above.
Customer supplied items control	Procedures should be set up to ensure the acceptance, storage and maintenance of all items supplied by the customer.
Change control management	Procedures for the control of change should be prepared, established, implemented and maintained.
Testing and formal qualification	Testability of the requirements should be established. Reviews of criteria, test procedures and documentation should be established. Any tools or data used in testing must be identified and verified.
Preparation for software delivery	Procedures must be established for the delivery of the software, and conformance to the original requirements established.
Software embedding and hardware integration	Compatibility of software and hardware must be established.
Access, accommodation and assistance	Facilities should be provided to allow the customer to check that all requirements have been discharged.

12.2.3 Improve the process

Many quality management systems get no further than the documentation stage. They do not change the practices and attitudes in place in the organization. For the process of continuous improvement to become part of the culture of the organization a number of factors are crucial:

- senior management must support and implement the process themselves;

- people have to want to change; therefore

- people have to see the need and the benefits.

The factors are those associated with any change in working practice and are the same whether we are introducing tools and methods or changing the whole process of the IT function. Staff acceptance is therefore vital (Fig. 12.3). This will not happen by itself.

Fig. 12.3 'Staff acceptance is therefore vital.'

The management of change is critical to the success of the process. The danger is that the introduction of a QMS by management will be seen as the imposition of new working practices (Fig. 12.4). The system can only work if staff perceive the benefits to themselves.

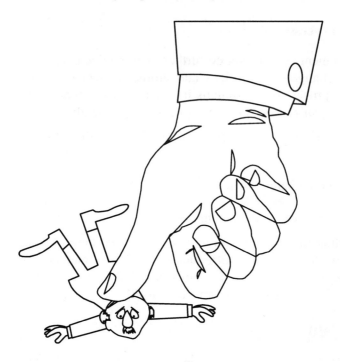

Fig. 12.4 The QMS may be perceived as an imposition.

These include the potential for:

• greater job satisfaction;

• less time spent on pointless activity;

• greater pride in work;

• more group participation; and

• more staff input into the way they do their job.

It is particularly important that communication is a two way process. For staff to be motivated, they must feel 'involved' and that their contribution and ideas will make a difference.

This is even more important when introducing a quality management programme than when introducing software engineering methods and tools, since the programme should involve a greater number of people in a variety of roles and departments. It is not sufficient for the IT function to want to change; they must convince the whole organization.

A tension exists in any organization where a quality culture is being established. The tension exists between a force acting from the top down and a force coming up from the bottom. The top down force is the 'desire to manage'. Management is absolutely necessary. It is not possible to achieve quality by committee. Without firm management, there will be no policy, no strategy, no consistency in decision making, and chaos will ensue.

However, there is a clear need to feed ideas up the organization. A quality culture will increase the flow of ideas from the work force. Strong management can verge on autocracy. What one person might regard as a well-organized stable environment may in fact be stagnant rather than stable. People with ideas which conflict with those of management can be seen as trouble makers. A perception that the last person to have an idea was sacked for it will not encourage others to come forward. There are no clear rules on this. Ask a well-regarded manager the principles he uses and he may well quote a set of ideas and statements. Ask how he does his job and he will probably use phrases such as 'by experience' or 'one instinctively knows'. Intuition ultimately plays a large part in managing people. This is unhelpful when trying to identify best practice. It is even less helpful when a badly regarded manager says the same thing!

A balance between structure, direction and policy on the one hand and innovation, lateral thinking and creativity on the other is required. Views of quality which emphasize conformance in components can too easily lead to an emphasis on conformance when dealing with staff. There is a time for doing things 'by the book' and a time for not. One of the best definitions of an expert is someone who knows when the rule book can be safely discounted.

The question to be considered in the context of CASE is whether it is better to introduce new methods and tools as part of an ongoing programme of continuous improvement in the whole process or whether it is better to establish each separately.

The risk in adopting an integrated approach is that the degree of change will simply be too high to be acceptable and effective. The alternative piecemeal approach runs the risk of benefits being unrealized due to problems elsewhere in the process.

Practical experience suggests that the introduction of a QMS has much in common with the introduction of a software engineering method.

Conceptually, this would appear to be the case as well. It is therefore suggested that these should be implemented as a single stage. Other activities such as automation of the method using a CASE tool or certification of the QMS to an external standard should be treated separately. This route offers the quickest return for the lowest risk. The second case study in this chapter describes how one company implemented SSADM and a quality management system leading to ISO9000 certification, but opted not to introduce a CASE tool as well.

12.3 THE ROLE OF STANDARDS: ISO9000 AND TICKIT

The same concerns which have led to increased adoption of structured methods and the adoption of CASE tools have led the UK Government to encourage software developers to establish quality management systems and have them certificated to the ISO9000/EN29000/BS5750 quality management standard (ISO, 1987). The standard establishes the model to be employed and then the accreditation body, e.g. BSI QA in the UK for the ISO 9000 series, is called in to ensure that the implementation meets the required standard and indeed continues to meet the required standard over time. In practice, three levels of accreditation are encountered, as summarized in Table 12.2:

Table 12.2 Types of accreditation.

Accreditation type	Description
First party	Internal monitoring only
Second party	External monitoring by a customer
Third party	External monitoring by an independent standards body

It is obviously more effective to have the quality management system accredited externally. The advantage of third party accreditation over second party accreditation is that the supplier only has to satisfy one accreditor. Clearly, to have to justify one's quality practices to six different customers is undesirable, in terms of cost and time expended. In the past, certain key customers have assumed almost third party status. For example, the defence industries in many countries, e.g. the UK MOD and the US DoD, are such key customers of software houses that their second party accreditation is accepted by many as a *de facto* standard. However, the ISO9000 series is now predominant and increasingly is replacing second party standards.

The series dates from 1979, when BS5750 was introduced in the UK. In 1987, the corresponding ISO, BS and EN standards were harmonized to produce three identical series of standards. In this text, we shall use the ISO numbers for consistency. The corresponding European and British standards are given in Table 12.3, which also lists the function of each standard.

Table 12.3 The ISO9000 series of quality management standards

ISO	EN	BS	Description
ISO9000	EN29000	BS5750 pt0	A guide to selecting the appropriate standard for a quality management system.
ISO9001	EN29001	BS5750 pt1	The specification of a QMS for design, development, production, installation and service.
ISO9002	EN29002	BS5750 pt2	The specification of a QMS for production and installation.
ISO9003	EN29003	BS5750 pt3	The specification of a QMS for final inspection and testing.
ISO9004	EN29004	BS5750 pt4	Guidance in setting up a QMS to meet the ISO9001/2/3 standards.

One of the biggest barriers to acceptance of ISO9001 amongst IT practitioners is its generic nature and its origins as a manufacturing standard. Although ISO9001 has been applied in many service and tertiary businesses, many IT people still feel it is inappropriate and difficult to apply. The response to this from the standards bodies is to issue 'notes for guidance' on the application of ISO9001 to software development.

It should be stressed that these do not supersede the standard, but rather amplify its contents with the aim of explaining how the standard should be applied in a software context. These notes, published in 1991, are known as ISO9000-3 (ISO,1991). ISO9000-3 headings are summarized in Tables 12.4 to 12.6 which give all the principal section headings and lists the corresponding clauses in ISO9001, classifying the degree of guidance provided as none, minor, significant or major.

ISO9000-3 has a target audience of the IT community. It is intended as a complete document in its own right, and its structure therefore differs from ISO9001. The structure of ISO9000-3 is as follows:

- Sections 1 to 3: Introductory material. The first three clauses of the standard are concerned with defining the scope of the standard, references to other standards and definition of seven terms as used in ISO9000-3.

- Section 4: Quality system – framework. This part contains four subsections: management responsibility, quality system, internal quality audit and corrective action.

- Section 5: Quality system – life cycle activities. This section contains nine sections, dealing with activities related to one or more parts of the life cycle. Many of the corresponding sections in ISO9001 seem insubstantial in comparison when applied to software.

- Section 6: Quality system – supporting activities. This section contains nine items which cover the remaining activities. Some, such as configuration management are mentioned only briefly in ISO9001.

Table 12.4 The ISO9000-3, Section 4: Quality framework

Sub-section	Sub-section title	ISO9001 clauses	Addition to ISO9001
4.1	Management responsibility	4.1	Significant
4.2	Quality system	4.2	Significant
4.3	Internal quality audits	4.17	Minor
4.4	Corrective action	4.14	Minor

Table 12.5 The ISO9000-3, Section 5: life cycle activities

Sub-section	Sub-section title	ISO9001 clauses	Addition to ISO9001
5.1	Contract reviews	4.3	Significant
5.2	Purchaser's requirements specification	4.3a , 4.4	Significant
5.3	Development planning	4.2	Significant
5.4	Quality planning	4.2	Significant
5.5	Design and implementation	4.4, 4.9	Significant
5.6	Testing and validation	4.10, 4.13	Significant
5.7	Acceptance	4.10, 4.1 3	Significant
5.8	Replication, delivery and installation	4.15	Significant
5.9	Maintenance	4.19	Major

Table 12.6 The ISO9000-3, Section 6: Quality system

Sub-section	Sub-section title	ISO9001 clauses	Addition to ISO9001
6.1	Configuration management	4.4, 4.5, 4.8	Major
6.2	Document control	4.5	Significant
6.3	Quality records	4.16	None
6.4	Measurements	4.20	Major
6.5	Rules, practices and conventions	4.9, 4.11	Significant
6.6	Tools and techniques	4.9, 4.11	Significant
6.7	Purchasing	4.6	Minor
6.8	Included software product	4.7	Significant
6.9	Training	4.18	Minor

The key areas of guidance provided by ISO9000-3 are requirements definition, life cycle definition, configuration management and measurements. Software is considered to be different from other applications because:

- it is considered as an intellectual object;

- the development process has its own characteristics and importance;

- replication always gives an exact copy;

- software does not deteriorate,

- once a fault is fixed it will not re-occur.

However, in spite of these differences, it is stressed by ISO that these 'notes for guidance' are not a new or different standard. Quality systems are still assessed against ISO9001. They are conceived as an aid to users of ISO9001 seeking to apply it in a software environment.

They are not intended to add to the requirements of ISO9001. Their scope is defined as providing guidance:

'...where a contract between two parties requires the demonstration of a supplier's capability to develop, supply and maintain software products.'

ISO (1991)

12.3.1 Do we need standards and third party accreditation?

Surveys of current practice make alarming reading. In a survey carried out in 1991, over 40% of companies claimed no quality assurance function at all (Davis *et al.,*1993).

The question asked was 'What type of quality assurance standard does your department implement?' The responses are shown in Fig. 12.5, where multiple responses are classified according to the most rigorous procedure employed.

In an earlier survey, Price Waterhouse (1988) found quality practice to be extremely variable and it was this that led to the establishment of the TickIT initiative to promote good practice in this area.

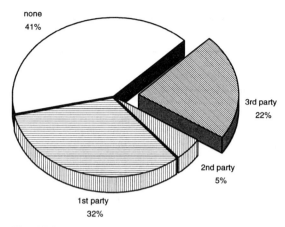

41%

3rd party
22%

2nd party
5%

1st party
32%

Fig. 12.5 Uptake accreditation by type of quality practice.

If we look at the percentage of companies with an externally certificated quality practice, then only 22% of companies in this survey had certification. The 1991 survey indicates that the take-up of certification is significantly greater amongst external software suppliers; i.e. those driven by market forces to demonstrate competence, or at least those required to have obtained the certification as a prerequisite of bidding for contracts. Of those companies which could be classed as software suppliers, 58% had externally accredited quality systems, whereas only 10% of the companies who used their software internally had externally accredited quality systems.

However, one would expect companies using software engineering methods and tools to be more 'quality aware' than the average. To examine this view, the respondents were classified according to the development method employed used. The results are shown in Table 12.7.

In all cases except one, practice exceeds that of the overall sample, indicated by dotted lines in Fig. 12.6.

Table 12.7 Quality practice amongst users of software engineering methods

For those using	*% with some QA* *(59% of all companies)*	*% with external certification* *(22% of all companies)*
SSADM	100	50
Yourdon	68	28
JSD	76	38
VDM	75	39
Gane/Sarson	73	40
O-O design	75	35
Prototyping	74	39
Data flow diagrams	62	20
Information engineering	64	26
Other methods	79	29

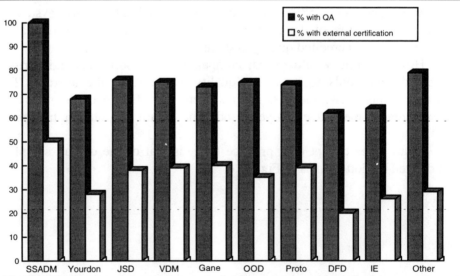

Fig. 12.6 Quality practice amongst users of software engineering methods.

Benefits claimed (Low, 1992) for companies to be derived from a third party accredited QMS include:

- Reduction in avoidable costs at all stages.

- Earlier error detection. The later an error is discovered, the more it costs to correct, and the less likely it is to be properly corrected.

- Greater likelihood of on-time delivery, leading to improved image with customers.

- More effective use of scarce staff. Better development of staff knowledge and skills, thus improving market values for the staff.

- Improved staff retention ratios: they prefer to be members of a team who 'have got the QA message'!

- Greater sense of professionalism, leading to easier recruitment because quality is attractive.

However, there is considerable scepticism about the short- to medium-term business benefits. For small to medium size companies the investment required is considerable. For those companies already investing in new methods and tools, the costs may simply be too high.

Quality management in the IT field is 'still very immature' (TickIT, 1991). With some national variation, this statement appears to apply to the rest of Europe. However, with the advent of the Single European Market (SEM) in 1992, there is growing pressure for accreditation to recognized international standards. In recognition of this trend, the UK Government has launched the TickIT initiative to boost awareness of certification issues and to increase levels of accreditation amongst IT firms in the UK. This programme is designed to promote the EN29001 standard together with the ISO9000-3 notes for guidance for software development.

It is easy to measure the effectiveness of such programmes by the number of firms achieving accreditation. It is less easy to quantify the overall effect upon software quality.

In general terms, the application of continuous improvement techniques and software engineering methods are complementary. Certainly, the methods and working practices are generally in sympathy, both being based upon a systematic process. However, the practical implementation, particularly of CASE tools, may not be so straightforward.

Rather surprisingly, many CASE tools do not provide the facilities needed to support a quality management system implemented in accordance with ISO9001 or ISO9000-3. In particular, almost all tools fail to provide adequate configuration management tools. They are also poor in the area of testing and auditability. It was reported to the authors recently that a software supplier accredited under the TickIT scheme had found only one CASE tool on the market which supported their quality management practices sufficiently to justify purchase.

12.4 CASE STUDIES

12.4.1 Company A

The company was established in 1987 to provide innovative technology-based training solutions, specializing in hypertext applications. Initially, a small team worked out of the local University's Centre for Software Engineering Technology but they are now an independent company based on the University Innovation Park.

Being a new and small company in a highly competitive marketplace, it was soon evident that success depended upon a 'quality approach' to products and services: providing what customers want on schedule, at agreed cost and right first time.

The first projects were large scale and high profile – a hypertext Guide to Glasgow for the Garden Festival and a training course on pcb components for an electronics company. For these it was necessary to use sub-contract programmers to complement the small team. This created many problems but in many ways this brought long term benefits because it highlighted many, many examples of what could go wrong!

One of the UK's leading life offices recognized that technology based training had a significant role to play in the growth and development of the organization. Against strong competition from large, long-established companies, the company won the contract to design and develop a training and information system for a large financial organization's branch network and head office training centre.

The system would initially run on stand-alone PCs with the option to be networked later. The success of this pilot project would determine the longer term plans for large-scale implementation of technology based training and for the establishment of an in-house development unit.

It was agreed that the first application would be induction training for new staff. The system would introduce trainees to the organization, their role and job function, the concept and history of life assurance and to the organization's products.

The client gave a high level of commitment to the project, making a significant investment in hardware and in people. Besides developing the first system, the company also helped recruit and train a team which would be responsible for maintenance and development of future systems.

It was essential that the company avoided stereotypical software problems: not knowing when the product would be complete, how much it would cost and how it would perform. A dramatic change in the initial specification could not be permitted mid-project. In addition, it was necessary to ensure that every member of the team worked to agreed standards, documenting every stage of design and production.

Hypertext systems have great potential to get out of hand, so solutions to these problems had to be found, as this was the project on which the company's reputation would be built.

The developers first sought the commitment of the 'subject expert' who took responsibility for the content of the 'courseware'. Once this was obtained, regular meetings were scheduled and procedures for recording changes to specification were agreed.

The team met on a regular basis and original time scales, costs and so on were reviewed at each meeting. Early identification of problems helped keep the project on track. Formal inspection of the system at each stage ensured that all parties fully accepted each component of the system. A structured design method was used to enable and ensure 'good practice'.

The method facilitated the following practices:

- A framework was defined, providing a step-by-step object oriented approach to the courseware. Aims and objectives were defined against which the design could be matched.

- The method provided an understandable illustration of how the courseware would be structured for the client and the development team.

- The method set a pattern for documentation, ensuring that every stage was documented and 'signed off' before progressing to the next stage.

- The method legislated against the temptation to work directly on screen before designs had been agreed.

- The method allowed extensive use of prototyping: vital to the client to see what they were getting.

- The method enabled meaningful communication between all parties.

Having agreed that there must be a systematic approach to the entire project, all aspects of this were implemented despite the many temptations to 'reverse engineer' the product.

Design techniques will document bad design just as happily as good design. Therefore, design alone is not enough; it takes commitment, the right culture and a supportive environment.

The benefits were apparent to the company and to the client. The company delivered, on time, a system of which they had 'ownership': there were no unexpected characteristics, they were familiar with its content, and it did what they wanted. Any minor changes which were required after rigorous testing by their analysts and users were made quickly and easily without serious repercussions for the system as a whole. The method gave the company and the client a good basic framework and procedure for future development, allowing new people to join the teams and work creatively but to an agreed standard.

In producing the system, a pattern of 'best practice' was established which enabled the company to refine and improve productivity. Encouraged by the success, the company is now moving towards automation of project management and documentation.

The system took nine months from initial discussion to final implementation. Following tests, there were two days to make fairly major changes to file structure as window handling problems became evident. At the time of writing, the system has been in full use throughout the company for some months. No system defects have been reported in that time.

The clients have several major projects under development and are now doubling the size of their team. The company is building on this early success.

12.4.5 Company B

The second company is part of a larger group supplying software to a range of markets in the public and private sector. The company supplies software to housing departments within local government.

The company became part of its current group in 1987. In 1988, the company went through something of a crisis. The local government market is driven by legislation. When a major new piece of legislation is introduced, e.g. the Housing Benefit Act, 1988, there is a major opportunity for the software suppliers to sell new systems to support the new regulations. However, timing is critical and time scales for development are often very short.

In 1988, the company were launching a new housing benefit system. The system had to be in place by April to satisfy the needs of local authorities considering new legislation coming into force then. To meet their obligations, the company was forced to release a product which was not properly tested and had some unfortunate errors.

Customer reaction was predictably unfavourable, and the company's image suffered accordingly. If the company was to remain in this market place, then a new start was required to regain customer confidence. It was decided to develop a new product with a new set of working practices, with the emphasis upon quality. The parent company made some changes to the management of the company and then made funds available for a new product.

The new regime was set out in the companies' service charter:

'The Service Charter outlines the company's commitment to quality products and services. The central element is a product and services guarantee. This guarantee means that services will be repeated if they do not meet customers' expectations. Ultimately, customers' money will be refunded if the company fails to address problems effectively. The move to provide this guarantee was a well-considered business decision. If deficiencies occur in our product or services, they cost us and our client money. We will not hide fault fixing charters under maintenance costs. This means we have the best possible structures to eradicate imperfections from our software and support services.'

The new product was an integrated management information system for housing departments. At the end of 1988, the company spent five months on a detailed investment appraisal, covering market research, product proposal, checkpoints, competition, risk analysis, technical analysis and financial analysis. This appraisal made estimates for the period up to 1990.

The company chose to use the full SSADM method. This proved popular with development staff. It was helpful both as a basis for consistent and effective working practice and as a vehicle for changing the whole ethos of the company towards the quality culture sought by the organization. However, a CASE tool was not used as this was considered to represent too much change and too high a risk. The system was developed using INGRES on Pyramid and then SEQUENT hardware. The production system was targeted at a range of UNIX hardware including machines from ICL and IBM as well as SEQUENT.

The software engineering method was only part of the holistic approach adopted, characterized by:

- Management involvement from the start of the project.

- Allowing sufficient time to develop and test the product properly, determined by development needs rather than short term commercial pressures.

- Use of a stable and experienced staff.

- Extensive training for the stable workforce.

- Extensive use of the PMW project planning tool.

- Introduction of team working practices.

The whole approach was based upon a quality management system and once the system was in place, certification under ISO9000 was applied for. By 1992, the whole operation had received certification for its quality procedures and the company was able to present itself to the world as a company that had very much put its house in order.

The first objective of the change in working practices and the introduction of SSADM was to deliver to the market place within carefully planned time scales a product that was reliable and would re-establish the company's reputation.

This objective was reached, with benefits arising in the coding and implementation stage from the use of SSADM at the analysis and design phases. The transition in working practice was assisted by the adoption of SSADM and a stable well-motivated workforce meant that training investment was retained.

The second question of re-establishing the company's reputation seemed to be a tough task at first. A degree of scepticism meant that many customers wanted someone else to take the risk and be first. However, as systems have successfully been installed, the scepticism has receded.

In terms of customer perception, there is little doubt that external certification of the quality systems has helped this process of building confidence. Inside the company, the process of external certification has caused little change, since the practices were already established and the certification process is regarded as a vindication of the process that the company had already been through.

12.5 SUMMARY

In this chapter we have explored the relationship between continuous improvement techniques and the introduction of tools and methods. We have shown how there are close links between the two and how the two may complement each other when carefully introduced. At the same time, warnings have been sounded regarding the dangers of too much change at one time. The key points are:

- Software engineering methods and tools are part of a broader process.

- The overall process is servicing the information needs of the business.

- To ensure that business needs are met, all parts of the process must function effectively.

- A quality management system documents a systematic process for all activities.

- To be effective, it must be accompanied by cultural change.

- ISO9001 is an international standard defined for quality management systems.

- ISO9000-3 provides notes for guidance on the application of the standard to software development.

- Many software producers have no systematic quality procedures.

- Many CASE tools do not provide comprehensive support for quality management systems.

FURTHER READING

Crosby, P.B. (1986) *Quality is Free,* McGraw-Hill, London.

Deming, W.E. (1986) *Out of the crisis,* MIT Center for Advanced Engineering, Study, Cambridge, Mass.

Juran, J.M. (1979) *Quality Control Handbook,* 3rd edn McGraw-Hill, London.

These are classic texts from arguably the three principal authorities in the field.

Gillies, A.C. (1992) *Software Quality: Theory and Management,* Chapman & Hall, London.

This text looks at software quality issues specifically, and combines software engineering with quality management ideas.

Oakland, J. (1989) *Total Quality Management,* Heinemann, London.

This is perhaps the best overview of total quality management.

13

When it works ...

13.1 INTRODUCTION

So far in this book, we have covered a series of case studies, each of which describes very different experiences that companies have had with the introduction of CASE tools and the development of IT systems. In the face of many overly optimistic views of the technology, this book has tried to point out some of the potential pitfalls and problems.

However, the purpose of this book has been to point out the pitfalls so that others may learn from past, often painful experiences. In this final chapter, the emphasis is on looking at the positive factors that have led to real business benefits where these have been realized. These do suggest that an effective and appropriate use of tools and methods can lead to significant gains for the business or organization concerned.

13.2 REASONS FOR SUCCESS

The case studies which have been expounded in the previous chapters of this book have contained several lessons concerning why a particular IT development may be successful. The main messages to be gleaned from these are outlined below:

- Methods can be very important, and extremely useful, in an IT development, and tools can be used to support these methods. It must, however, be remembered that the tools are for support, and that training in both methods and tool use is vital to the success of the project.

- Methods come before tools, and total commitment to the method (and use of the tools) is vital.

- Change should be made in an evolutionary, iterative and gradual manner, and revolutionary change is a recipe for disaster.

- People factors are the most important in any scenario. It is the people in any organization that will make the introduction of CASE tools a success, or otherwise.

- Get staff commitment. This is vital to the success of any project. Commitment must be present at all levels in the organization. It is particularly important that the senior management is totally committed to the introduction of any methods and CASE tools.

- Staff training in the use of CASE is essential for success. Enthusiasm will quickly turn to frustration if staff cannot achieve what they wish because of a lack of specific skills.

- Productivity may not arise immediately on the introduction of methods and/or CASE, but it must be realized that great benefits will result in the long term. Cost justification is, of course, very important but may be difficult to put together as a result.

- Consultants can be very useful and can, indeed, be the making of a successful project. However, you must be careful to get the correct consultant for the job. Communication between the consultant and the staff of the company is a key issue.

13.3 PROBLEMS

There are a number of problem areas in relation to the success, or otherwise, of tools and methods.

13.3.1 Adoption

The costs of software 'spoilage' that were given in a 1988 report for the Department of Trade and Industry (DTI, 1988) were extremely high. In that year, it was estimated that amongst software produced by UK suppliers and sold to UK users, more than £500M p.a. were being wasted due to poor quality software.

This wastage could be accounted for in terms of:

- low productivity

- project over-runs

- error correction

- unnecessary maintenance.

It was further estimated that if the total lifetime costs were taken into account the software 'spoilage' costs would be £1000M p.a. for the sector. This figure is equal to the cost charged for the software on delivery!

More detailed facts regarding the use of systematic methods and CASE tools have been obtained from analysis of the data collected from the survey undertaken by Stobart *et al.* (1991b) referred to in Chapter 4. The survey showed that only 18% of respondents were actually using CASE. A follow-up questionnaire to a selection of the non-respondents indicated that the major reason for non-replies was that their organizations were also not using CASE. Hence, the true use of CASE at the time of the survey was probably well below 18% – possibly as low as 6%!

The survey data also provided useful information on the use of systematic methods in the sector. The majority of organizations who were actively using CASE were also using systematic methods. These probably represent the more technologically aware companies. However, there are a large number of companies who are neither using CASE or methods. Analysis of survey data on code development techniques and methods also confirmed that many organizations had failed to adopt software engineering approaches.

A fundamental problem in the adoption of new technologies is a lack of clear unbiased information.

The people who have the best information are the vendors. They are not likely to provide an objective view. Academics have the time to consider a variety of methods and tools but little first hand practical experience. Practitioners are generally too busy coming to terms with the technology to feed back information. Failures are some of the most informative examples but pride and company prestige often prevent these coming to light. At least one company declined to provide a case study for this book because of the delicate situation between them and their CASE tool supplier.

A problem often cited is that the rate of change is such that information is quickly out of date. Some readers may well feel that the case studies in this book are less relevant already because of the time to reach print.

However, one of the principal messages which emerges from this book is that the keys to success are good management, good working practice and a good understanding of the problems both of the nature of software development and of the business to which the software is to be applied. This is true whichever method or tool is to be employed. It was true in 1988, 1993 and will still be true in 1998.

13.3.2 Methods

The major problems associated with the adoption of cost effective and systematic development methods are:

- The current wide range of methods that are available and the lack of experienced staff.

- Unwillingness of organizations to accept change and adopt any new 'standardized method'. In many cases this is simply due to the costs, primarily in staff time, that are incurred with any major change.

- Unwillingness by software developers themselves to accept and adopt changed working practices.

- The uncertainty of the long term future of particular methods and the possibility of a European Standard method.

- An unwillingness to consider and accept differing methods, if an organization has already invested heavily (and in some cases very heavily) in methods of its own.

- Biased pressure to adopt the methods and related tools promoted by suppliers and consultancy organizations.

- A lack of high quality material to support technological information transfer between the developers of methods and the intended practitioners of the methods.

13.3.3 CASE

The prospective market for CASE tools has been confused by the large variety of different products that are available. In an attempt to clarify matters tools have been categorized in an attempt to more accurately describe their functions. Unfortunately, tool vendors and manufacturers have not totally standardized on what these terms mean, so such categorization has simply added to the confusion, and not removed it!

The other major problems are:

- The current high cost of CASE tools. These costs were given as a major reason for not adopting CASE by the respondents to the survey by Stobart *et al.* (1991b). The actual cost of CASE (per staff member) appeared to be approximately double what non-CASE users were willing to spend.

- The high costs for extra hardware and initial staff time in the adoption of CASE.

- Lack of management support to invest in and use tools (and related methods).

- Unwillingness of staff to adopt new working practices.

- The possibility that if an organization is not adopting good development practices, the introduction of CASE may simply allow the development of bad software more quickly!

- Some tools are of too general a nature to be of any significant benefit whilst others are so dependent on a particular method that adoption of the tool means that the organization must also adopt a method which itself may not fully satisfy its needs.

The solution to overcoming these barriers lies in adopting a clear strategy based upon a sound financial case. With senior management commitment to the strategy and commitment from the staff themselves, the goals will be attained and a successful outcome reached.

13.3.4 Human problems

In the adoption of methods and tools there can be major problems with staff at all levels. People do not like change, especially if it is a possible threat to their livelihood or the way in which they have to work. Computing professionals are like everyone else in this respect. Managers lack confidence in their ability to understand and control the new technology, whilst designers and production staff may believe that the methods and tools will destroy the artistic and creative aspects of their work.

It is true that adoption of the new technologies has a large impact on working practices and that many members of staff have been unable (or are unwilling) to alter their working practices. This 'Luddite approach' has greatly contributed to the high rejection of the technology in the commercial and administrative sector.

Just as some staff are unwilling to accept change, there are others who will. However, their expectation of what the new technology can offer may be too high. They are convinced that there will be overnight improvements in all areas of their software development. This is, of course, untrue, since the real benefits are in the long term. The non-fulfilment of their expectations leads to dissatisfaction and an unwillingness to use the technology in earnest.

The reaction of many staff will depend upon the way that the new methods and tools are implemented. People often resent the manner in which things are done rather than the deed itself. Where change is concerned, people are often particularly insecure and suspicious. The sophistication of CASE tools is such that automation and semi-automation of software development will make staff more skilled not less.

13.4   CASE STUDIES

The following case studies illustrate the benefits that can accrue from a successful implementation of CASE tools and methods.

13.4.1 A strategy for improved productivity in system development

The company concerned is one of the most innovative financial services companies in the world. It is the holding company for companies which transact life insurance and pensions business, and manage unit trust and offshore funds, and property investment and insurance broking services. The company has, from its earliest stages, adopted data processing as a key element in its management strategy.

The undoubted success and subsequent growth of the company have led to an increasing requirement for IT resources to support the demand for information systems. The company currently has 280 staff engaged in systems development and maintenance, and overall computing power running at 44 MIPS, with 60 gigabytes of disc storage capacity.

This demand for IT resources has stressed the need for adherence to time scale and cost considerations which are critical to product profitability, forecast launch dates and the creation of competitive advantage. Against this background, the company has approved a strategy of using software engineering to improve systems development productivity.

Consideration was given to the types of systems requiring development over the next 3–5 years, and the likely methods to be used, such as bespoke, package, end user computing, etc. were predicted. A productivity strategy appropriate to the needs of the business was formulated, and its objectives are:

- to deliver systems faster and cheaper;

- to maximise effective user involvement;

- to promote a consistent approach to systems development;

- to remove technical complexities from the process;

- to reduce development workload on mainframe computers.

These objectives were to be achieved by automating the development process using wherever possible networked PC based tools. Intercommunication needs between the development team members and the company highlighted the necessity for PC networking, avoiding the use of high-priority and heavily loaded mainframes, whilst retaining mainframe access when essential.

Five possible options for PC networking were identified and assessed against a list of required functions, leading to the selection of Banyan for extensive trials over a four month period with stringent conditions including:

- tests of all communications paths envisaged;

- a volume test running 40 PCs on one file server;

- links via the Local Area Network (LAN) to the existing computers;

- testing a variety of PC software and system development;

- software.

The network software and hardware worked well, with some links being smoother than others. The majority of problems were concerned with the unavailability of networking versions of certain packaged software, necessitating their use only at the PC level (but storing the results on the file server). As software engineering methods are introduced, the organizational responsibility for implementing the networks amongst all development staff needs to be determined.

One aspect of the development process being automated on the network was programming. Prior investigation and testing of structured programming led to the conclusion that difficulties were caused by the lack of expert support and tools which would simplify drawing and maintaining program structure diagrams. The introduction of two automated tools by the vendors of Jackson Structured Programming (JSP) gave facilities not previously available and led to the decision to pilot test structured programming.

It was envisaged that the introduction of a PC based programmers' workbench would enable new programs to be developed, compiled and tested before their introduction on the mainframe. A major factor was the necessity to increase the productivity and quality of COBOL programming, and it was intended to link the corporate data dictionary into the workbench to automate the production of the COBOL data division.

The PDF (program development facility) is a PC or mainframe based tool used to enter and amend JSP program structures in diagrammatic form. Operations and condition lists are produced as a result of JSP program design. PDF then uses this input to generate automatically the schematic logic of the COBOL procedures division in the form of pseudo-code. The other program divisions can also be input through PDF.

JSP-COBOL is a PC or mainframe based pre-compiler which takes PDF data and generates COBOL source code. The PC based compiler/editor, CICS emulator and Animator from Microfocus were selected to link into the Jackson tools on the basis that there are interfaces to, and capabilities for working with, JSP tool and Excelerator, and on its level of market penetration.

This was treated as a high-priority project with a defined time scale and end date. The discipline enforced by the fixed end date was extremely important, in that failure to adhere to the time scale caused by the learning curve led to the creation of a time backlog which had to be reduced by subsequent productivity gains.

The first stage involved the introduction of the JSP technique using PC based PDF and mainframe based JSP-COBOL. This was expedited by the assistance of a JSP expert from the internal development centre in training, on-the-job education and support of the largely inexperienced staff engaged on the project, which was the development of a sales force administration system on a Unisys system.

The second stage involved the development of a valuation system for the Life Actuarial department using PC based PDF, JSP-COBOL, Microfocus compiler, editor, CICS emulator and Animator and the Banyan network. This was targeted for use on the Amdahl system, with support again from the development centre.

Comparison of programming productivity by an independent review body on the initial project gave positive results, leading to the conclusion that it would be reasonable to expect gains of:

- up to 10% using JSP;

- up to 17% using PDF;

- up to 15% using JSP-COBOL.

As a result, 80% fewer programming errors and 25% fewer design faults had occurred. Once completed, the valuation project was reviewed by an independent body whose main (subjective) findings were:

- All JSP tools worked without difficulties once initial incompatibilities between the PC compiled COBOL and the mainframe compiler were fixed by Microfocus.

- The animator improved confidence in program testing.

- Control over the versions of programs compiled to the mainframe was improved by having only one person with access to DOS facilities to copy from the Banyan.

After initial scepticism, the evaluation team members endorsed most strongly the use of JSP supported by software engineering.

13.4.2 System development for a record company

This case study is based on the experiences of a computer consultancy and software house formed in 1985. The two founders of the company had previously held senior executive posts in a major UK software house and knew a lot about developing commercial mainframe systems, but not so much about other hardware and software platforms.

The company's forte is to evaluate customers' needs and to provide packaged or bespoke systems to meet these needs, including the use of new methods and tools such as CASE.

The company recognizes that the most difficult area to get right in the whole of IT is establishing what it is that the user really needs. The user always knows that he/she has a problem and hence a requirement, but defining that in terms that mean the same to computer professionals is not easy. CASE can go a long way to solving this problem.

The company has worked with major corporates in financial, retail and manufacturing industries in diverse application areas. These include securities trading, consumer complaints, order processing, distribution etc. The majority of these developments are undertaken in relational databases such as ORACLE, Ingres and Informix in UNIX environments and in Synon/2 on the IBM AS/400.

The company aims to deliver quality, which is measured in terms of value for money. The intent is to provide the user with a robust, flexible, documented system that will meet their business needs for a reasonable fee.

To meet this aim, development tools are used together with disciplines embodied in their standards. Productivity tools are used to maximize value for money: the savings gained must outweigh the initial cost of the tool over its lifetime. The overall cost includes education and training and a few inevitable mistakes along the way.

This case study focuses on their experience of using CASE, relational databases and 4GLs in particular by profiling one project. The experiences gained across a number of projects are, however, relevant, particularly in the areas of education for both computer and user staff.

The project to be looked at in detail is a system to calculate copyright revenues for a record company. The tool used in the project was Synon/2.

Synon/2 is variously claimed as a Computer Aided Software Engineering tool (CASE), a Fourth Generation Language (4GL) and a code generator. The company's view is that it is not a full CASE tool as it does not provide the all-embracing aids provided by full CASE tools. However, it does have elements of CASE about it; it certainly is close to a 4GL and it generates either RPGIII or COBOL code. It works as a design tool by the use of Action Diagrams and provides standard functions which are then used to generate code with no further intervention.

The company undertook a trial in collaboration with a client, sharing the cost of education and training. Four staff members were selected for training: one senior analyst/programmer, two analyst/programmers, all three of whom knew RPGIII and, lastly, an analyst/programmer who knew other 4GLs but had had no experience of RPGIII. The immediate success stories were the senior analyst/programmer who could see the drudgery being taken out of the job, and the analyst/programmer without RPGIII. The others had a tendency to examine the code being generated and to feel they could better it.

Experience with other 4GLs suggested a fairly long elapsed time before staff become proficient and this proved to be the case. However, enough was learnt from the initial trial to see two aspects clearly:

* There are savings to be made by using Synon/2 instead of RPGIII, in both actual and elapsed time.

* The code produced by Synon/2 is robust and reduces testing time.

Synon/2 was subsequently used with other clients on major developments, one of which is discussed below.

Towards the end of 1988, the company was asked to tender for a development to calculate the royalties due on the use of copyright material for a record company. The copyright department kept a record of sixty thousand songs on index cards and wished to move this on to a computer for copyright calculation purposes. In addition to the maintenance of these titles, they also required flexible searches so that new record and disc albums on a particular theme could be compiled.

The consultants were not involved in the preparation of the functional specification, which had been prepared by a competitor on the basis that the system would be developed in RPGIII on an IBM System/38. Towards the end of the functional specification phase the record company decided that the development should be undertaken in Synon/2 and selected a number of companies with Synon/2 expertise to tender, for a fixed price. The consultant company won the bid, not because they were the lowest price but because they were able to demonstrate experience with, and knowledge of, Synon/2.

The development was complex and estimated at 5 man years work to be completed in about 10 months. The project was managed very tightly. Not everyone on the team had Synon/2 experience and, indeed, the team leader herself was new to the product. The project was divided into a number of distinct phases, but to begin with the data model had to be reworked and the team had to satisfy themselves that the design was sound. This is an essential part of any 4GL development. More time must be spent at the outset getting the design correct. It is not impossible to change it later, but benefits are only fully realized when design changes are minimal.

Work was started on the reference file maintenance, which is an area in which Synon/2 is very powerful. One task estimated at 70 days in RPGIII took a newly trained graduate with no previous computing experience, just 15 days to complete. The next stage was the transaction processing, another area where Synon/2 is good and the team gradually built up confidence.

The user was very co-operative. It had been pointed out in the tender that it would be necessary to compromise on screen design to obtain the benefits from Synon/2. Certain items appear in fixed positions and although they can be changed, doing so would negate Synon/2's automatic code generation. The user accepted all the screen designs without complaint. There were, however, some difficulties relating to the functional specification with the original intention for the development to be undertaken in RPGIII. The processing of data files would have resulted in cumbersome screen usage for the user and therefore, in a couple of instances, RPGIII was employed to meet functional requirements. This was only done after discussions with Synon themselves to explore alternative solutions.

The batch programs gave some difficulty, as did the reports. There were a number of large calculation programs that contained complex requirements. These may well have taken just as long to complete in Synon/2 as they would have done in RPGIII.

Standards were set at the start of the project and quality assurance procedures ensured that regular checks were made on adherence to standards, general understanding of Synon/2, etc. Staff were supported by an experienced Synon/2 consultant and this was found to be valuable, if not essential, for newcomers to the product.

On delivery to the record company, the system was subjected to acceptance test trials. The system went live and the user was satisfied. They have the system that they require with no major problems and very few minor ones.

There were a few problems with two or three areas on performance but fortunately these could all be corrected easily by using a different Synon/2 function and changing the environment on the AS/400.

It is perhaps arguable whether Synon/2 is a CASE tool or a 4GL. However, this is not really the issue. The company has used Excelerator on other developments and are currently evaluating the link between the two products. The important message is that there are undoubted benefits to be gained through using tools such as Synon/2. Effort is increased at the design stage of a project but decreased during the build phase.

Maintenance is easier, faster and therefore cheaper. The use of a product such as Synon/2 can save between 25% and 30% of development time and should result in an easier to maintain system.

It isn't cheap. However, any organization that is faced with £250 000 of new development over a four year period will gain by using a tool as sophisticated as Synon/2: that figure includes the education and training costs. Looking at specific points, there are a number of management issues. Firstly, management has to make a commitment to using Synon/2. It is often said that the best way to start using Synon/2 is on a small non-urgent project. However, this leaves the trial in the hands of the technicians and will, by its non-urgent nature, ensure that management does not give it very high priority. Urgently required high profile projects readily attract management commitment!

Management also has a role to play in educating users. Whatever 4GL is used, it is vital that the organization is committed to it and that users will be trained to expect longer time in design and less flexibility with screens and reports, in return for lower costs and higher quality. Business analysts should know what the tool will do – and what it will not do. That way the business analyst can influence the user over screens and reports and general benefits provided by such new tools.

13.4.3 Quality in real-time systems

The company in this case study has been in existence for nine years and now employs around 150 people. The company has a number of departments, including one which carries out essentially fixed price project work for the nuclear, petrochemical and automation industries. Quality, delivery and cost are the key parameters which determine the success of a development project and ultimately result in the company's good name.

Understanding new customer requirements and expectations is one of the most complex aspects of the company's operation. Operating under a quality system, there is an obligation to present a certain minimum amount of design information to a pre-defined presentation standard. This can create difficulties when attempting to be competitive. Clearly flexibility is required on the part of the quality system. Engineers must take on board experience gained with previous projects, whilst maintaining a clear image of the expectations of the project.

It is vital to understand the scope of a project but it is also important to gain insights into the quality of the customer! Key factors which affect confidence are the size and constitution of their project team, their own knowledge of the requirements, the views of any third parties who may be involved and the customers' understanding of future needs. All these factors need to be evaluated along with the more 'conventional' matters of hardware and development teams.

Variation control is an area of great concern to managers and several mechanisms have been set in place to ensure compliance with customer requirements. Regular technical design reviews, carried out by the project team and led by an external moderator, can highlight danger areas both in terms of lack of definition and potential project overrun. The use of a formal testing scheme with supporting fault reporting systems for all stages of code testing maintains good records of the evolution of the application.

Fault reporting is particularly relevant to customer witness testing. Two main problems occur during this phase. Once the system is operational, one may find that the customer suddenly realises that the system is missing some operational attribute which has been overlooked from the inception of the project. However, the greatest number of requests for variation come from such things as graphics layouts, reports generation etc. It has been found that a simple 'pro forma' to police change requests coupled with good and simple layout of design documentation ensures a sound basis for negotiating contract amendments.

Sizing a computer system, particularly where memory upgrades involve total redesign of the core processing system, is a vital part of the initial design. Thus, two techniques have been developed for ensuring that the system is adequately specified. The primary technique for assessing program size is for each member of the team to read all the available design documentation and to attempt to code (even on paper) some representative sample. By assessing and scaling those development times, the resulting code size can be estimated. A secondary method, often used in simple sequential applications, is to base memory requirements on the amount of inputs and outputs required to carry out the control of the system.

Modular design is a fine design goal. Implementing 'modules' of software in environments which do not readily support such an approach adds some interesting problems to development. A mistake sometimes made by development teams is to divide an application into rigorous vertical segments based on the Function Design Specification. Thus one module will control product make up, another might control reaction etc.

As can be seen, application development is really a matter of selecting the correct vertical or horizontal model and then impressing the programming team with the importance of the application model and ultimately monitoring their progress as detailed above.

Maintaining progress can cause problems of projects which have time scales which stretch beyond a couple of months. It is therefore vital to establish deliverables (usually through the planning system) which can be seen in a week or two.

The transition to using Yourdon design tools came about as a mix of customer requirement and a personal decision by the management team that a better way of visualizing the application was required.

Initially, great doubt was raised about the suitability of the method to real time applications and whether a 'real' software engineer could generate and/or understand all these diagrams.

A mixture of product evaluation against a real application and training provide a key in unlocking the virtues of the system.

Once a customer (who was thankfully happy to take on board the Yourdon concept) had seen the reduction in development time and, more importantly, had realized the enhanced visualization which the data flow diagrams and state charts provide, the developers could proceed with some confidence that the system would work in other applications.

The great benefit which Yourdon gave to both customers and the programming team was that it acted as a bridge between the customers' process views of system operation and the programming view. This bridging can also be thought of as a way of adding formality to a design and indeed it was surprising how quickly bottlenecks and omissions in understanding of an application could be identified.

A further benefit (which was highlighted by the real time nature of our applications) was the ability of data flow diagrams to segment event based sequence control and alarm interlocking from continuous data processing functions. This in turn adds a subtle 'modularization' to the software which is useful in establishing neat code areas within the actual program.

In summary, the use of Yourdon has added a further layer of quality to the development procedure. While requiring some learning and re-thinking of an application by the customer and the supplier, it does ultimately yield consistent and functionally correct software.

The company's current long term development aim is to integrate Yourdon fully into the company, which will require staff training and ultimately a series of 'awareness' sessions for their customers.

The company were, at the time of writing, working on a series of 'rules' for the presentation of Yourdon which will enable the direct mapping of data flow diagrams, state diagrams and data dictionaries to executable code.

13.5 SUMMARY

This chapter has focused upon three success stories. They have demonstrated many of the lessons from the rest of the book. They have shown how the use of tools and methodologies can help speed up the development of a quality IT product. They have demonstrated that in these specific cases:

- methods such as JSP and Yourdon led to a successful IT development and can help developers make large productivity gains;

- CASE tools were very useful for the support of such methods.

They have also shown the importance of many of the factors highlighted earlier:

- The many benefits of the new software engineering technology can only be achieved if it is implemented and used correctly. If development staff are uncommitted or fail to recognize the benefits that can follow from systematic and automated software production, then the technology will fail.

- No matter how advanced the technology becomes, without good organizational attitudes it can do little to help surmount the many difficulties that currently face systems development staff. Only full acceptance of the technology by both management and staff will result in success.

- The correct technology must be adopted. There is a clear need for accurate and meaningful information regarding its use. For these new developments to be accepted within commercial organizations, there needs to be much better means of efficient and effective technology transfer, and it is perhaps this area that needs to receive a high priority.

- If particular methods and tools are to be accepted and used there must be a much better understanding of them, their use and the actual benefits which they can bring. The underlying cause for several of the problems which have been identified is simply fear of the unknown coupled with a lack of unbiased, easily accessed information. To overcome such problems we need to create enabling mechanisms which will facilitate technology transfer and mutual understanding.

For the future, there are implications for the training and education of IT graduates:

- Are these graduates equipped with the knowledge to enable them to operate as effective software engineers within the commercial sector?

- Do their courses provide them with the necessary professionalism that should be expected?

- How do they compare in these areas with graduates in the more traditional engineering disciplines?

14

Final thoughts

In this book we have tried to present the experiences of companies who have implemented software engineering methods and tools with varying degrees of success. We have also tried to draw out the lessons from those experiences. From the many messages given there are two principal messages which seem to occur repeatedly:

- CASE methods and tools have the potential to address problems or create them. As powerful tools they can make a significant difference either way. This is the pneumatic drill versus hammer argument. The pneumatic drill is a much better tool for digging holes in the road, but used incorrectly it will make a bigger hole in your foot!

- The difference between success and failure is not principally about technology at all. The secret of success is good management. So if you are waiting for software engineering salvation don't wait for the perfect CASE tool to come along, but look at your processes, see how they may be improved and develop an implementation strategy which will almost certainly involve the methods discussed and may include use of a CASE tool.

Bibliography

REFERENCES

Ashworth, C. and Goodland, M. (1990) *SSADM : A Practical Approach*, McGraw-Hill, London.

Awad, E.M. and Lindgren Jr ,J.H. (1992) Skills and personality attributes of the knowledge engineer: an empirical study, *Proceedings IAKE'92 Conference*, IAKE, New York.

Boehm, B. (1981) *Software Engineering Economics*, Prentice-Hall, New York.

Barker, R. (1990) *CASE Method: Tasks and Deliverables*, Addison-Wesley, Wokingham.

CCTA (1990) *SSADM Version 4 Reference Manual,* NCC-Blackwell, Manchester.

Chikofsky, E.J. and Rubenstein, B.L. (1988) CASE: reliability engineering for information systems. *IEEE Software,* **5** (2), 11–16.

Constantine, L.L. and Yourdon, E. (1979) *Structured Design*, Prentice-Hall, New York.

Crosby, P.B. (1986) *Quality is Free,* McGraw-Hill, London.

Davis, C., Gillies, A.C., Smith, P. and Thompson, J.B. (1993) Current quality assurance practice amongst software developers in the UK. *Software Quality Journal,* **2** (3), 145–161.

DeMarco, T. (1979) *Structured Analysis and System Specification*, Prentice-Hall, New York.

Deming, W.E. (1986) *Out of the Crisis,* MIT Center for Advanced Engineering Study, Cambridge, Mass.

Edwards, H., Thompson, J.B., and Smith, P. *The STePS Method*, To be published by McGraw-Hill, London, 1994.

Ernst & Young (1992) *The Landmark MIT Study: Management in the 1990s*, Ernst & Young, New York, USA. p.4.

Finkelstein, C. (1989) *An Introduction to Information Engineering – From Strategic Planning to Information Systems,* Addison-Wesley, Sydney.

Fisher, A. (1988) *CASE : tools for software development,* Wiley, New York.

Gane, T. and Sarson, C. (1977) *Structured Systems Analysis: Tools and Techniques*, McDonnell-Douglas, St Louis.

Gilb, T. (1988) *Principles of Software Engineering Management,* Addison-Wesley, Wokingham.

Gillies, A.C. (1992a) Modelling software quality in the commercial environment. *Software Quality Journal*, **1** (3), 175–191.

Gillies, A.C. (1992b) *Software Quality: theory and management,* Chapman and Hall, London.

Gillies, A.C.(1993) LOQUM: locally defined quality modelling. *Total Quality Management* (in press).

Hart, A.E. (1989) *Knowledge Acquisition For Expert Systems,* Chapman & Hall, London.

Hughes, C. and Clark, J. (1990) CASE: the reality of current utilization, *Journal of Information System Management,* **3** (3).

ISO (1986) *Quality Vocabulary*, ISO8042.

ISO (1987) ISO9000–9004, from BSI in the UK.

ISO (1991) ISO9000–3, from BSI in the UK.

Jackson, M.A. (1975) *Principles of Program Design*, Academic Press, London.

Jackson, M.A. (1983) *System Development,* Prentice-Hall, London.

Juran, J.M. (1979) *Quality Control Handbook,* 3rd edn, McGraw-Hill, London.

Kirkham, J.A. and Stainton, C. (1992) An analysis of the DTI SOLUTIONS programme. *The ITI Papers*, **3** (3), 25–31, IT Institute, University of Salford, Salford, Manchester M5 4WT.

Kliem, R.L. and Ludin, S.L. (1992) *The PEOPLE Side Of Project Management,* Gower, USA.

Lantz, K.E. (1989) *The Prototyping Methodology*, Prentice-Hall, New York.

Lehman, M.M. (1990) Uncertainty in computer application and its control through the engineering of software. *Journal of Software Maintenance,* **1** (1), 3–28.

Longworth, G. and Nicholls, D. (1986) *The SSADM Manual,* NCC-Blackwell, Manchester.

Low, C. (1992) TickIT, getting the message across, in Solomonides, C.M., Kirkham, J.A., Bowker, P. and Gillies, A.C., SOLUTIONS Case Studies. *The ITI Papers*, **3** (1), IT Institute, University of Salford, Salford, Manchester, M5 4WT.

Low, G.C. and Jeffrey, D.R. (1991) Software development productivity and back end CASE tools. *Information and Software Technology*, **33,** (9), 616–624.

McCall, J.A. *et al.* (1977) Concepts and definitions of software quality. *Factors in software Quality*, NTIS, **1.**

Myers, G.J. (1979) *The Art of Software Testing*, Wiley, New York.

Naur, P. *et al.* (1976) *Software Engineering: Concepts and Techniques*, Petrocelli/Charter, New York.

NCC (1990) *PRINCE Manual,* NCC-Blackwell, Manchester.

Oakland, J. (1989) *Total Quality Management,* Heinemann, London.

PACTEL (PA Computers and Telecommunications) (1985) *Benefits of Software Engineering Methods and Tools*, Department of Trade and Industry, London.

Parkinson, J. (1990) Making CASE work. in Spurr, K. and Layzell, P. (eds), *CASE on Trial*, Wiley, New York.

Peters, T, (1988) *Thriving on Chaos*, Macmillan, London.

Peters, T. and Waterman, R, (1982) *In Search of Excellence*, Harper and Row.

Price Waterhouse (1988) *Software Quality Standards: The Costs And Benefits,* Department of Trade and Industry, London. (Survey results cited in Gillies (1992b) above).

Price Waterhouse (1990) *Information Technology Review 1989/90*, Publications Office, Price Waterhouse, 32 Bridge Street, London, SE1 9SY, p. 19.

Price Waterhouse (1992) *Information Technology Review 1991/92*, Publications Office, Price Waterhouse, 32 Bridge Street, London, SE1 9SY, p. 7.

Rock-Evans, R. (1991) *CASE Analyst Workbenches: A Detailed Product Evaluation, Volume 4*, Ovum Ltd, 7 Rathbone Street, London, p. 47.

Salford University Business Services Limited (1991) *Software Engineering Solutions: Final Report*, Department of Trade and Industry, London.

Simpson, H. (1986) The MASCOT method. *Software Engineering Journal*, **5**, 103–120.

Solomonides, C.M., Kirkham, J.A., Bowker, P. and Gillies, A.C. (1992) SOLUTIONS Case Studies. *The ITI Papers*, **3** (1), IT Institute, University of Salford, Salford, Manchester, M5 4WT.

Sommerville, I. (1989) *Software Engineering*, 3rd edn, Addison-Wesley, Wokingham.

Spikes Cavell (1993) Software methodologies. *Computing*, 8 April, p.20–21.

Sprouls, J. (1990) *IFPUG. Function Point Counting Practice Manual Release 3.0,* IFPUG, Westerville, OH, USA .

Stacey, R.D. (1990) *Dynamic Strategic Management for the 1990s,* Kogan-Page.

Stobart, S.C., Thompson, J.B. and Smith, P. (1990) An analysis of the use of commercial CASE tools. *4th Int. Workshop on CASE,* California.

Stobart, S.C., Thompson, J.B. and Smith, P. (1990) An examination of the benefits and difficulties that the implementation of a software development environment can present within the DP industry. *International Conference on System Development Environments and Factories,* Berlin.

Stobart, S.C., Thompson, J.B. and Smith, P. (1991) CASE: software development. *IEE Computer-Aided Engineering Journal,* **8** (3), 116–121.

Stobart, S.C., Thompson, J.B. and Smith, P. (1991) The use, problems, benefits and future directions of CASE in the UK. *Information and Software Technology,* **33** (9),629–636.

Taylor, J.R. (1989) *Quality Control Systems,* McGraw-Hill, London.

TickIT (1991) *TickIT: Making a Better Job of Software,* Department of Trade and Industry, London.

Warnier, J.D. (1981) *Logical Construction of Systems,* Van Nostrand Reinhold, New York.

Yourdon, E.N. (1989) *Modern Systems Analysis,* Prentice-Hall, New York.

FURTHER READING

Adeli, H. (Ed.) (1992) *Heuristics, The Journal Of Knowledge Engineering,* IAKE, **5** (5).

Bader, J., Edwards, J., Harris-Jones, C. and Hannaford, D. (1988) Practical engineering of knowledge-based systems. *Information and Software Technology*, **30** (5).

Batarekh, A., Preece, A.D., Bennett, A. and Grogono P. (1991) Specifying an expert system, *Expert Systems With Applications*, **2** (1), Pergamon Press, Oxford.

Biggelaar, J.C.M. den (1992) An integrated Master's course in Knowledge Engineering. *Proceedings IAKE'92 Conference*, IAKE, New York.

Bleazard, G.B. (1976) *Program Design Methods*, NCC-Blackwell, Manchester.

Born, G. (1988) *Guidelines for Quality Assurance of Expert Systems,* Computing Services Association.

Buxton, J.N., Naur, P. and Randell, B. (Eds) (1969), Software engineering techniques. *Proceedings NATO conference (Rome, Italy, 1969),* published by the Scientific Affairs Division, NATO, Brussels.

CCTA (1983*) Central Government Mandatory Standard No. 18,* Parts 1– 6, Central Computer and Telecommunications Agency, London,

Clanon, J. (1992) Developing Knowledge Engineers at Digital Equipment Corporation 1982 – 1992, *Proceedings IAKE '92 Conference*, IAKE, New York.

Cupello, J.M. and Mishelevich D.J. (1988) *Managing prototype knowledge/expert system projects, computing practices.* Communications of the ACM, **31** (5).

Cutts, G. (1987) *Structured Systems Analysis and Design Methodology*, Paradigm Press, London.

Dahl, O-J., Dijkstra, E.W. and Hoare, C.A.R. (1972) *Structured Programming,* Academic Press, New York,

Edwards, J.S. (1991) *Building Knowledge Based Systems – Towards a methodology*, Pitman, London.

Eva, M. (1992) *SSADM Version 4: A User's Guide*, McGraw-Hill, London.

Gomaa, H. (1986) Software development for real-time systems. *Communications Of The ACM*, **29** (7), p 657 – 668 .

Gorney, D.J. and Coleman, K.G. (1991) Expert system development standards, *Expert Systems With Applications*, **2**, Pergammon, Oxford.

Hall, P.A.V. (Ed.) (1990) *SE90: Proceedings Of Software Engineering 90*, Cambrige, UK.

Harmon, P. and King, D. (1985) *Expert Systems – Artificial Intelligence In Business*, Wiley, Chichester.

Hekmatpour, S., and Ince, D., (1988) *Software Prototyping, Formal Methods and VDM*, Addison-Wesley, Wokingham.

Hickman, F.R. (1989*) The Pragmatic Application Of The KADS Methodology,* The Knowledge-Based Systems Centre Of Touche Ross Management Consultants, London.

IEEE (1983) *IEEE Standard Glossary of Software Engineering Terminology, IEEE Standard 729–1983*, IEEE, Washington, USA.

Ince, D. (1991) Software Quality and Reliability: Tools and Methods, Chapman & Hall, London.

Jones, G.W. (1990) *Software Engineering*, Wiley, Chichester.

Macro, A. and Buxton, J. (1987) *The Craft of Software Engineering*, Addison-Wesley, London.

Mair, P. (1987) Integrated project support environments. *Electronics and Power*, **33** (5), 317–323.

Martin, J. and Finkelstein, C. (1981) *Information Engineering*, Savant Research Studies, Carnforth.

Martin, J. (1982) *Program Design Which is Probably Correct*, Savant Research Studies, Carnforth.

McGraw, K.L. and Harbison-Briggs, K. (1989) *Knowledge Acquisition – Principles and Guidelines,* Prentice-Hall, New York.

Mellor, S.J. and Ward, P.T. (1986) *Structured Design for Real-Time Systems,* Yourdon Press, New York,

Naur, P. and Randell, B. (Eds.) (1969), *Software Engineering: Report on a Conference Sponsored by the NATO Science Committee* (Garmish, Germany, October 7–11, 1968) published by Scientific Affairs Division, NATO, Brussels.

Olphert, C.W., Poulson, D.F. and Powrie, S.E., (1990) ORDIT: the development of tools to assist in organizational requirements definition for information technology systems. *Conference Proceedings Computer, Man and Organization II,* May 9–11, Nivelles, Belgium.

Porter, D. (1992) *Towards The Common KADS Method,* Touche Ross Management Consultants, London

Price Waterhouse, (1988) *Software Quality Standards: The Costs and Benefits,* Price Waterhouse Management Consultants, London,

Ratcliff, B. (1987) *Software Engineering: Principles and Methods,* Blackwell, Oxford.

Regnier, L., Robert, J-M., Dalkir, K. (1992) How Do Knowledge Engineers Work?, *Proceedings IAKE '92 Conference,* IAKE, New York.

Smith, P.(1992) Knowledge Engineering Education In The UK – A Perspective, *Proceedings IAKE '92 Conference,* IAKE, New York.

Spurr, K. (1989) CASE: a culture shock, *Computer Bulletin,* 1, (5), 9–13.

Stamps, D. (1987) CASE: cranking out productivity, *Datamation,* July 1, 55–58.

Stevens, W.P., Myers, G.J. and Constantine, L. (1974) Structured design. *IBM Systems Journal,* **13** (2), 115–139.

Thompson, J.B. and Edwards, H.M. (1990) Analysis and design methods for computer based information systems – the impact of the post-1992 single European market, *European Trade and Technology Conference ETT'90*, Sunderland, UK.

Thompson, J.B. (1989 and 1990) *Structured Programming With Cobol and JSP*, Volumes 1 and 2, Chartwell Bratt, Bromley, UK.

Tuthill, G.S. and Levy S.T. (1991) *Knowledge-Based Systems: A Manager's Perspective*, Tab Books, London.

Warnier, J.D. (1977) *Logical Construction of Programs*, Van Nostrand Reinhold, New York.

White, M. and Goldsmith, J. (1990) *Standards and Review Manual For Certification In Knowledge Engineering: Handbook Of Theory and Practice*, Systemsware Corp, New York.

Index